PLAYS FROM
AFRICAN FOLKTALES

PLAYS

FROM AFRICAN FOLKTALES

WiTH iDEAS FOR ACTiNG, DANCE, COSTUMES AND MUSIC

by **CAROL KORTY**

illustrated by **SANDRA CAIN**

music by **SAKA ACQUAYE** *and* **AFOLABI AJAYI**

CHARLES SCRIBNER'S SONS  *New York*

AUTHOR'S NOTE

The plays in this book do not attempt to represent material from specific African ethnic groups. My sources were many, and I have mixed and adapted elements in order to create a balance of plot lines and characters that would work dramatically and would reflect the spirit of humor and humanity common to so much of African folk literature. I hope the result may spark others to seek out more material from African heritages.

1 3 5 7 9 11 13 15 17 19 H/C 20 18 16 14 12 10 8 6 4 2

PRINTED IN THE UNITED STATES OF AMERICA
Library of Congress Catalog Card Number 74-24418
ISBN 0-684-14199x

Dedicated to the spirit of play in all of us

CONTENTS

ABOUT THIS BOOK

The four plays in this book are based on African folktales. There are hundreds of these tales. Originally they were made up to teach people important things about the place where they lived, such as which plants and animals were good and which were dangerous, and about the way to get along in their society. The stories were also meant to entertain, for no one would want to listen to all those lessons if the listening weren't fun. They were made up so long ago that no one knows, for certain, who started the original story ideas. Each time a story was told, some parts of it changed, because in traditional African storytelling, the storyteller put something of himself or herself into the tale. The storyteller also added details about the people who were listening, and he invited the listeners to dance, sing, or add ideas of their own. So, while the basic action of the story remained the same, there could be as many versions of it as there were tellers and listeners.

The plays in this book are my own versions of some African tales that I especially love. I read them and then put them together in a way that I felt would be good for a group of actors to do the telling. I hope you enjoy reading them and that you'll want to act them out. If you do, I hope you'll put something of yourself into them, and, if you have listeners, that you'll make your audience feel you're doing it especially for them.

At the end of the book are suggestions for acting, dance, music, and costumes. You may want to use these ideas with other plays as well. Perhaps you'll feel like making up your own plays from other tales or from things that have happened to you or things you've seen or imagined.

Many wonderful people helped me shape these plays. Some of them are Ken and Joan Jenkins, Paul and Jessie Treichler, Bill Pendergrast, Sandra Cain, Richard A. Miller, Afolabi Ajayi, Saka Acquaye, Alex Page, Anita Page, and Sasha Page. There were also student actors, professional actors, colleagues, and audience members too numerous to name. I am grateful to all of them for their ideas and energy, and for making the work such fun. Thanks also to Antioch College, the Danforth Foundation, and the State University College of New York at Brockport for their financial and institutional support.

CAROL KORTY

SOME WAYS TO USE THE SCRIPTS

There is no one way to work with any script, so don't worry about whether or not you're doing it the right way. You can present the four plays in this collection as separate, individual plays or, by using the interludes, you can perform them as a group. After you've read them to yourself, try reading them aloud with other people, each taking different parts. Some of you might read them aloud while others do the acting out. Try the action realistically, or as a dance, or as a shadow play. You could do a pantomime or mime show, where everything is made clear through movement alone and no words are spoken.

Six of you could handle all the parts, if you double up. However, there are enough parts in the four scripts for more than twenty people. If you want to involve even more people, have a crowd of villagers and a flock of pigeons instead of one or two and use extra musicians, dancers, and singers. Some of the main animal characters are referred to as Mr. because in the traditional tales they are male. But these parts can be played by either boys or girls or changed to female characters, if you prefer.

These plays can be performed very simply, without scenery, costumes, masks, dance, or music. But you will need a few stage properties, or props. You can use real objects, like bowls, food, feathers, or nuts, or artificial objects made from papier-mâché or cardboard cut-outs. Or you might want to mime or pantomime the objects. The section on mime (page 94) will help you with this.

The Narrator in these plays is like a storyteller or host, creating a feeling of fun and participation for everyone. He or she can conduct the interludes between the plays, the opening, and the closing, involving the audience in the spirit of the plays. He can also be a musician and coordinate any music you want to use with the acting and dancing. However, you may not always want to use a Narrator, and in that case, the things he tells the audience about the characters can be made clear through action alone. The actors can create the feeling of welcome and good fun by the way they perform.

STAGE TERMS

Actor or Player—a person who acts out things with his or her body and/or voice.

Character—a person, animal, or object who exists in the play and is brought to life by the actor.

Director—the person who helps the actors get the play ready to perform and coordinates all those who are contributing music, costumes, or scenery.

Dialogue—words spoken by the characters in a play.

Stage directions—the instructions written by the playwright describing the characters and the physical setting on stage. Stage directions help the actors bring the play alive. They are set off from the dialogue by italics.

A script—the words of a play written by the playwright, including dialogue and stage directions.

A play—a term sometimes used to mean a script but usually meaning the whole event of acting out and performing the words of a script. Plays can also be made from ideas that are never written down in a script. They can be made up or improvised at the moment they are being performed.

Improvising—making up things right on the spot without practice. You can improvise acting, dance, or music. When performers improvise, they are creating much or all of their own material without help from a playwright, a choreographer, or composer.

Rehearsing—the practicing done by actors, dancers, and musicians to get ready for a performance.

Miming or Pantomiming—imitating real life actions, using imaginary objects as though they were really there or using your whole body to act out things other than people, such as animals, machines, or rain, or acting out all or part of a play silently, without dialogue.

Stage—the place where the action of a play is rehearsed or performed. It can be the stage in an auditorium or any open space that actors set aside to use as the performing area. It might be in a classroom, an empty lot, a back yard, or on a porch or stoop.

On stage—anywhere within the performing area.

Off stage—the place just outside the performing area, usually out of the audience's sight.

Props—an abbreviation for properties. These are objects the characters use in the action of the play. Hand props are objects small enough to be held by the actors. Bigger pieces, such as chairs or tables, are called stage props or set props.

Scenery—the things used to dress the stage or performing area. It might be drapes or designs that create an interesting atmosphere. Or it could be things that make the stage seem like a particular place, a kitchen or a forest, for example. These things can be real, such as a refrigerator, or artificial, such as a painted cardboard tree. Stage props are part of scenery.

14

PLAYS FROM
AFRICAN FOLKTALES

THE OPENING
(optional)

In performing these plays as a group, you may want to start the telling by having the Narrator and actors enter with a lively dance. This will introduce your group and set the mood with sound, color, and movement. Once the dance is over, the Narrator greets the audience and the story part of the play begins.

THE MAN
WHO LOVED
To LAUGH

*Based on a tale from the Nuer people
of southern Sudan.*

CHARACTERS

MAN
WIFE
BULLY SNAKE
LITTLE SNAKE
ANT VOICE 1
ANT VOICE 2

DOG
MOSQUITO VOICE
RAT
THE CHIEF
VILLAGER(S)

G G G

PROP LIST

(These things can be real or mimed.)

HAND PROPS

yellow feather
work tools
bowl and spoon
food
broom

STAGE PROPS

stool
sleeping mat
shutters
door
grain barrel

NARRATOR: Hello! We'd like to tell you a story. And
if this story is full of lies, may the bells in my
mouth refuse to ring. *(He puts his index finger
in his mouth and pops his cheek three times.)* It
is a story about a man who loved to laugh.
*(MAN enters laughing with a little walk-about,
gives greeting, and exits. NARRATOR or musicians can accompany all such walks with a
drum beat.)*

There is a wife,
*(WIFE also enters with a little walk-about, gives
greeting, and exits.)*

and some snakes,
(SNAKES leap on fighting and hiss off.)

some ants that you can hear,
(ANT VOICES chatter off stage.)

but they're too small to see; a dog,
(DOG runs on and off again wagging eagerly.)

a rat,
(RAT darts on, sees audience, and darts off.)

and a mosquito. There he is now.
*(MOSQUITO VOICE buzzes from off stage. NAR-
RATOR watches the imaginary flight. He sees*

mosquito land on him and swats. MOSQUITO VOICE *registers the slap and buzzes away limply.)*

Missed him!
(THE CHIEF and VILLAGER enter.)

Oh, yes, and a chief and a villager.
(CHIEF and VILLAGER greet audience and exit.)

Let's start at the beginning with the man who liked to laugh.
(MAN re-enters laughing and does his walk-about or little dance. He is an easy-going person of large, loose movement style.)

Yes, he loved life, and he loved to laugh. He was happy with the world and with the people in it.
(WIFE enters and approaches MAN. She is sweet, young, and newly wed. She has a small delicate movement style.)

He was happy with his wife. And she was pleased with him.

WIFE: Why are you laughing?

MAN: I am laughing because the sun is shining, because you're pretty to look at, and because I love you.

NARRATOR: She was very pleased, and she said:

WIFE: That is very nice!

20

(MAN and WIFE do a walk-about together.)

MAN   *(stopping their walk).* It is time for me to go to work in the field.
(They do a turn-about, WIFE exits, and MAN starts his walk to the field.)

NARRATOR: When he came to the field, he found two snakes fighting there.
(BULLY SNAKE and LITTLE SNAKE leap on and fight in dance form. The small one is getting badly beaten.)

MAN   *(running between SNAKES).* Stop! Stop! I don't know how this started, but it had better stop fast for this little snake will be killed. *(He separates them and chases the large one.)* Get out of here, you bully! *(BULLY SNAKE exits.)* *(MAN continues his walk.)*

LITTLE SNAKE   *(in weezy, magic voice).* Wait! I want to thank you.

MAN   *(turns with great surprise and laughs).* I just thought I heard a snake say, "Thank you!"

LITTLE SNAKE: Yes, I want to thank you, young man . . .

MAN: What?

LITTLE SNAKE: . . . and to give you a present. Come here, son.

MAN: Well, I'm glad I could help you. *(Stops and laughs.)* But I'm absolutely amazed that I can hear you talking to me, and that I can understand you.

LITTLE SNAKE: You were kind to me. I want to give you a magic yellow feather. *(Presents him with large yellow feather.)* With this charm you will always be able to understand what animals say.

MAN: What a wonderful idea! This is a really beautiful charm. Thank you very much.

LITTLE SNAKE: I'm happy that you like it. But here is a warning! You must not tell anyone I have given you the feather, and you must not tell anyone about the new power it gives you.

MAN *(good naturedly).* All right, if you wish. I promise not to tell anyone.

LITTLE SNAKE: It is important. Because, if you tell, you will die.

MAN *(startled).* Oh, thank you for the warning. I'll be very careful. I certainly don't want to die. *(Considers.)* I don't want to die? No, I don't want to die because I love being alive, and I know I would miss it.
(MAN *spins about with feather, while* LITTLE SNAKE *does its snake-about.)*

22

NARRATOR: Then the snake said:

LITTLE SNAKE: Good-bye, dear friend. *(Crosses paths with* MAN.*)*

NARRATOR: And the man said:

MAN: Good-bye, dear friend. *(Moves around* SNAKE.*)*

NARRATOR: And they each went their separate ways.
(They complete the walk-about together, and LITTLE SNAKE *exits.)*

MAN: What a happy present! *(Laughs.)* I am just amazed. A snake has just spoken to me and given me a present. A magic yellow feather!
*(*MAN *puts feather in his pocket.)*

ANT 1 *(*ANTS *are off-stage voices.)* Watch out, for heaven's sake!

ANT 2: A monster!

MAN: Where's that? *(Looks about anxiously.)*

ANT 1: Quick, hurry.

ANT 2: I'm running as fast as I can.

ANT 1: Over this way. Quick.

ANT 2: Oh, no! There's another part of him.

MAN: What's happening? Who's talking? Where's the monster?

(He moves his feet, and ANTS *exclaim loudly.)*

ANT 1: Stop running and hide.

ANT 2: Hide? Hide? Where?

ANT 1: Under this rock. Quick.

MAN: Rock? There's no rock here. *(Looking at the ground.)* The ground is absolutely flat.

ANT 1: Whew . . . It's good it was here. Grass is no good at a time like this.

MAN *(looking down at grass).* There's no monster here either.

ANT 2: Keep still now and watch for him to leave.

MAN *(looking down at a spot near his feet).* It's ants! *(Laughs.)* Ants! There they are, hiding under a pebble. *(Laughs.)* And I am the monster. How strange people must look to them from underneath. *(Laughs.)* I've heard ants talking!

NARRATOR: Then he did his work in the field.
*(*MAN *begins his work. His work can be acted out with real stage props, such as a hoe, or a shovel, or pantomimed with imaginary objects; it can also be done like a dance to a drum beat.)*

And when it was finished, the man went home to his wife and to his dinner.
*(*MAN *exits or circles while* WIFE *and* DOG *enter to establish the house.)*

NARRATOR: When he came to his house, his dog ran out to greet him. (DOG *barks and runs wagging up to him.*)

MAN *(patting dog).* I am hungry, hungry, hungry!

WIFE: Good. I've made a special dinner for you.

NARRATOR: So he sat down to eat it.
(MAN *sits and eats.* WIFE *moves away and begins to sweep.*)

DOG: Don't be so greedy. (MAN *is startled.*) If he eats so fast, there'll be nothing left for me. He looks like an old goat.
(MAN *finally realizes that it is the* DOG *speaking. He laughs and chokes.*)

WIFE: Goodness, what's the matter?

MAN *(starts to tell her and stops, remembering that he must not).* Nothing . . .

WIFE: You choked on the food . . . (MAN *hands* DOG *some meat from his bowl.*) . . . and now you feed it to the dog. Isn't it good? I tried to cook it just right so you'd like it.

MAN: No, no. The food is delicious, my love. I choked because I was laughing.

WIFE *(reassured).* What made you laugh?

MAN *(again he starts to tell and remembers he cannot).* Nothing.

DOG: I take it back. He doesn't look as much like an old goat as I thought.
(MAN *laughs again.*)

WIFE: There you go again. What is it?

MAN: Wh . . . I thought of something funny.

WIFE: What was that?

MAN: I can't say really.

WIFE   *(helpless and perplexed)*. Can't say? You mean you won't say! I think you're making fun of me.

MAN: No, I'm not making fun of you. *(Goes to soothe her.)* Don't worry. It's not important. Let's not talk about it. It's time to sleep.

WIFE   *(calmed and loving)*. Please fasten up the door and shutters. I want to close the grain barrel and put this food away. *(WIFE does these tasks. The activities can be mimed or done with real objects.)*

MAN: All right. *(To DOG.)* Out you go, friend. You've had enough to eat. It's time to sleep.
(He shoos DOG outside and closes the door and shutters. DOG curls up outside door. WIFE prepares bed or sleeping mat, and they lie down. The activity should be carefully timed so actors finish together.)

NARRATOR: It grew quiet in the house until:

MOSQUITO   *(this character is an off-stage voice).* Bzzzzzzzzzz.

DOG   *(snapping at* MOSQUITO*).* Leave me alone. Can't you see I'm trying to sleep? It's much too dark to be out flying around.

MOSQUITO   *(buzzing).* Don't worry. I'm not after you. I want to get inside to take a good mosquito bite of that lady's arm. I saw her today, and she really looks juicy.
(MAN, *who has been overhearing the conversation, bursts out laughing.)*

WIFE   *(stirring).* Laughing again!

DOG: The place is shut up tight. You can't get in now. You'll have to wait till the morning.

MOSQUITO: No, in the daytime she swats at me. I have to get her while she's sleeping.

DOG: I'm in no mood to argue. You'll never get in there with those shutters closed. Now get out of my ear. I want to sleep.
(MAN *laughs again.)*

WIFE: What is making you laugh? Everything's quiet except for a few insects buzzing outside. *(Drops off to sleep again.)*
(MAN *gets up, goes to window, and opens shutters.)*

MOSQUITO: Oh, here's my chance. See you later, Dog. Bzzzzzzzzzz.
(MAN *watches the* MOSQUITO *enter and slaps his hands together to catch it.* MOSQUITO*'s stunned buzz lets us know he's received the blow. He buzzes away weakly.* MAN *looks at* DOG, *laughs, and closes shutters.*)

WIFE   *(wakening at the slap and laughter).* What are you doing, and what is so funny?

MAN: Nothing, really. Ah . . . some thought just struck me funny.

WIFE: You said before that some thought struck you funny, but you won't say what you're thinking. I'm sure now that you're making fun of me.

MAN: Really I'm not. Please don't be angry. Why would I want to make fun of you? Don't think about it any more. *(He pats her reassuringly and lies down again.)*

NARRATOR: The man really didn't want to laugh again, so he tried very hard not to think about the things he'd heard. Then he finally went to sleep. And his wife went to sleep. And the dog went to sleep. *(*MAN, WIFE *and* DOG *snore in turn.)* It grew quiet again . . . except for . . .
(RAT *comes running on right in front of* DOG, *sees* DOG *sleeping, turns on heel, and exits. Reappears pretending to be very casual.)*

28

RAT: Good evening.

DOG *(waking with a start)*. Evening.

RAT: Ah . . .

DOG: Looking for something?

RAT: Just out for a walk.

DOG: Good. Keep right on walking. No rats allowed. I'm on guard.

RAT *(tries new approach of being confidential)*. Actually, I'm out looking for a little grain.

DOG: Oh?

RAT: Do you happen to have any?

DOG: Yes.

RAT: Where?

DOG: Inside.

RAT: Can I have a handful?

DOG: No!

RAT: Please. Just a handful. Look how small my hand is.

DOG: The people are sleeping inside. Can't wake them up.

RAT: Please.

DOG: Come back tomorrow!
(RAT *starts to protest.*)

DOG: Come back tomorrow!

RAT   (*starts to exit and spins around with a new scheme*). How do I know you won't eat it before tomorrow?

DOG: Oh, me . . .

RAT: But I could come back tomorrow, and you'd say there was no grain left.

DOG: For heaven's sake! I never touch the stuff.

RAT: Oh, then you won't mind if I take a little.

DOG: Oh, get out of my hair! Go on; take a little.
(MAN *has been listening. He gets up and is on hands and knees ready to meet* RAT. RAT *leaps up to run to the door.*)

DOG: Don't use the door. Use the hole in the wall and be quiet!
(RAT *runs in through hole and stops dead still when he sees* MAN *is looking at him nose to nose. He spins around and runs out.* MAN *goes and gets the broom.*)

RAT   (*to* DOG). There's a man in there!

DOG: There's a man in there. Of course there's a man in there! Didn't I tell you he's sleeping and not to wake him up?

30

RAT: Sleeping?

DOG: Yes! Go on and be quiet.
(RAT *crawls back in.* MAN *is holding broom over his head, ready to hit the* RAT. RAT *stops short at* MAN*'s feet, slowly looks up his legs until he sees the* MAN*'s face, slowly looks down again, turns, and starts to sneak away.* MAN *bangs down the broom. A drum beat can give additional emphasis here.* RAT *makes a lightning-fast exit past* DOG, *who looks up with surprise.* MAN *laughs heartily.*)

WIFE (*waking with crash of broom*). What's going on?
(MAN *continues laughing.*)

WIFE: What are you doing with a broom in the middle of the night?

MAN (*thinking quickly, starts to sweep*). I'm just tidying up the house a little.

WIFE: Ohhhhhh . . . of all the insults! You get up in the middle of the night to check up on my work!

MAN: There was just a little grain on the floor . . .

WIFE: First you spit out the food I cook for you, and now you say I keep such a dirty house that you can't even lie down to sleep until you've cleaned it up!

MAN: No, love. You're wrong. Please don't be upset.

31

WIFE *(in tears)*. How can I not be upset when you act like this?

MAN: I would like to explain, but I'm not allowed to. I never meant to insult you. I love you very much. Please believe me.
(They each lie down.)

NARRATOR: That was all they said that night. They both felt very unhappy *(each turns over deliberately)*, but they finally went to sleep. In the morning the wife jumped up early and said:

WIFE: It's time to get up. I want you to come with me. *(She opens shutters and door and shoos away* DOG, *who exits.)*

MAN: What's the matter? Where are you going? Let's eat breakfast.
(He gets up sleepily.)

WIFE: I won't eat breakfast this morning, and I'm not going to fix it either. I don't want to spend another day in this house with you mocking me. I'm going to the Chief to ask him to settle this matter.

MAN: The Chief!

WIFE: Come on. *(Exits or circles to village.)*

MAN: Woman . . . ! *(Follows her.)*
*(*CHIEF *and* VILLAGER(S) *enter, establishing the village.* MAN *and* WIFE *enter.)*

NARRATOR: When they arrived in the center of the village, the wife found the Chief.

(The CHIEF *stands or sits in a position to show his authority.* VILLAGER(S) *are there as witnesses or assistants.)*

*(*MAN *and* WIFE *exchange a formal greeting with the chief to show their respect.)*

WIFE: Chief, I have come about a dispute: a matter that needs your settlement.

CHIEF: What is it?

WIFE: My husband mocks me.

CHIEF: Mocks you? How?

MAN: I do not. I would never mock my wife because I love her.

WIFE: He laughs at me. When we're alone, suddenly out of a silence, he bursts out laughing, and then he says it's nothing. He laughs when I give him food. He laughs when we sleep at night.

CHIEF   *(to* MAN*).* How do you explain yourself?

MAN: I am not laughing at my wife. But I cannot explain. I've promised not to tell the reason. *(*WIFE *moves away from him to stand near* CHIEF.*)*

VILLAGER: Why can't you tell? Are you ashamed of your reason?

MAN: No, my reason is a good one. But I'm not allowed to give it.

CHIEF: If it is a good reason, you can give it. If you refuse to give it, your wife will be taken away from you. She does not have to live with someone who makes fun of her. I will send her back to her own village to live with her parents.

MAN: Oh, Chief, please don't do that. I don't want to lose my wife. I love her very much.

CHIEF: This is my answer. Either you tell us the good reason for your laughter, or your wife will be returned to her father. *(To* VILLAGER.*)* Is this just?
*(*VILLAGER *nods assent.)*

MAN *(turning aside to think).* I would rather be punished for telling my secret than to have to lose my wife, so I will break my promise and tell. *(To* CHIEF.*)* Chief, I saved a snake from being killed. He thanked me and gave me a present, a magic yellow feather. *(Takes feather out of his pocket and shows it. All are amazed.)* With this charm, I can understand animals when they talk. Their tongues make me laugh. If you could only . . . *(He starts to laugh and collapses in the middle of his laughter.)*
*(*WIFE *rushes to help him but finds him lifeless. She is stunned.)*

VILLAGER: He is dead.

CHIEF *(amazed)*. Dead?
> *(WIFE begins a dance lament with keening, a wailing done by mourners. CHIEF and VILLAGER(S) join her, moving their heads, bodies, and arms in slow circles. While they dance, LITTLE SNAKE enters unseen from off stage and approaches MAN.)*

LITTLE SNAKE: Young man, I warned you not to tell. You once saved my life, but now my gift has cost you yours.
> *(Keening continues softly.)*

> I did not wish it to happen. *(Coils around MAN, who begins to stir.)*

VILLAGER *(noticing LITTLE SNAKE)*. Look at that snake!

LITTLE SNAKE: I know you had good reason.

WIFE: What is he doing?

CHIEF *(signaling all to stand back from MAN and LITTLE SNAKE)*. It is his charm. Do not interfere with things you do not understand.

LITTLE SNAKE: Your love is strong. We need your love and your laughter, so I will help you this time. Wake up, dear friend.
> *(MAN sits up laughing and sees LITTLE SNAKE who picks up the feather.)*

LITTLE SNAKE   *(interrupts* MAN *and gives him the feather).* It is yours, but do not betray the secrets that it gives you. Enjoy them through your laughter.
*(*MAN *continues his laughter and* LITTLE SNAKE *exits.)*

WIFE: He's alive!

VILLAGER: He's alive and he's laughing!

WIFE: Laugh all you want, husband.

CHIEF: Laugh all you want, and no one will ask questions.

WIFE: And when you laugh, love, I will laugh with you.
(All do brief dance or walk-about and exit laughing. LITTLE SNAKE *re-enters at the very end in time to catch the eye of the* MAN *before he exits.)*

FIRST INTERLUDE
(optional)

Interludes are a good place to have fun doing extra things for the audience. While the actors change the scenery for the next play, they can be accompanied by drumming and music. The actual changing of the set can even be made into a dance. Balance the kind of activity you plan for each of the interludes so they have variety and build up interest and anticipation for the play to come.

MR. HARE TAKES MR. LEOPARD FOR A RIDE

There are many trickster tales in West African folk-lore. Mr. Hare is a favorite figure in the Hausa culture of Niger and Nigeria. He is the granddaddy of our American Br'er Rabbit.

CHARACTERS

MR. HARE   MR. LEOPARD
                    MRS. LEOPARD

PROP LIST

(These things can be real or mimed.)

HAND PROPS

stick
rope
bucket or some other
   object for Mr.
   Leopard's activity

STAGE PROPS

box, stool, or raised
   level for Mr. Hare
   to sit on and from
   which to mount
   Mr. Leopard

NARRATOR: One day Mr. Hare was sitting out in front of his house.

MR. HARE *(sitting, twiddling his foot with a very nonchalant, ho-hum air).*
Hey, ho, what do you know,
What will I do today, today?
What will I do today, I say;
Oh, what shall I do today?
(MR. LEOPARD rushes by carrying something. It could be a bucket which he brings back filled or emptied on the return trip, or any other object to show he is taking care of business.)

MR. HARE *(leaps up delighted).* Good morning, Mr. Leopard! How are you?

MR. LEOPARD: Grrrr . . . *(Throws a glance over his shoulder as he hurries off.)*

MR. HARE: Very nice friend! *(Calls after him.)* You can't even stop long enough to say, "Hello." I don't know why I'm surprised. The only time you are ever friendly to me is when you think you might be able to trick me and catch me for your next meal. Well, it hasn't worked yet. I'm too fast for you. *(Returns to sitting and twiddling.)* Hey, ho, what do you . . .
(MR. LEOPARD hurries back again.)

MR. HARE *(leaping up).* Hey! What do you know! Greetings, again, Mr. Leopard!

MR. LEOPARD *(charges across to exit without pausing to notice* MR. HARE*).*
Grrrr. . . .

MR. HARE: Right in front of my door he passes, and not even a nod! He knows I'm safe on my own territory, so he won't bother with me at all. Not even a nod. *(Calls after* MR. LEOPARD.*)* That's not right! Just because you're big, you should not be rude. At least you can say, "Hello," even if you don't chase me.
*(*MR. LEOPARD *again rushes past, barely missing knocking over* MR. HARE.*)*

MR. HARE *(brightly).* Hello! *(Looks after him; realizes it's too late and shrugs, sitting down again.)*
Hey, ho, what do you know?
What will I do today . . .
Today! *(He jumps up.)* I know exactly what I'll do today. I'll do something to make that leopard notice me, *(looking at audience)* and I don't mean as something to eat!
(He hunches over and walks in a little circle with hands behind his back—or does a similar kind of activity to show he's scheming. He stops and continues to think aloud.)

If his house is that way *(points to* MR. LEOPARD *'s first entrance)* and he ran that way *(points to* MR. LEOPARD *'s exit, then looks at audience)*, it means he's not at home.

(He repeats the circling or his activity for thinking. Stops.)

I think I'll just take a little walk over to his house and leave a little message.

*(*MR. HARE *sets out with stylized walk or hopping sequence for long distance running. Drum can accompany him, increasing in intensity as he progresses.* MR. HARE *circles stage area, or does some other type of running, using entrances and exits to indicate that distance is being covered. He ends where* MRS. LEOPARD *has come out to establish her house.)*

MR. HARE: Hello there, Mrs. Leopard.

MRS. LEOPARD *(very attentive and very polite).* Greetings, Mr. Hare.

MR. HARE: How are you today?

MRS. LEOPARD: Fine, just fine, thank you. How are you?

MR. HARE: To tell you the truth, I'm not very well.

MRS. LEOPARD *(concerned).* Oh, I'm sorry to hear that, Mr. Hare.

MR. HARE: Is Mr. Leopard home by any chance?

MRS. LEOPARD: No, he left this morning to go hunting.

MR. HARE: Oh, that's too bad. I needed to use him.

MRS. LEOPARD: Needed to use him? *(Not understanding.)* What do you mean by that?

MR. HARE: I'm not feeling well, and I want to go to a doctor. It's too far a walk for me feeling this poorly. I thought Mr. Leopard could give me a ride.

MRS. LEOPARD *(more perplexed)*. What do you mean, "Give you a ride?"

MR. HARE: Well, I don't have a horse to ride, so I thought I would ride Mr. Leopard instead.

MRS. LEOPARD *(shocked)*. Ride Mr. Leopard! Are you crazy, you little rabbit?

MR. HARE: Hmmmmmm, no. I'm sure I could do it.

MRS. LEOPARD *(very worried)*. It's a good thing for you he isn't around to hear you say that. He'd eat you up in a minute for being so insolent.

MR. HARE *(reassuring)*. Oh, I doubt that. *(Very pointedly.)* Besides I know I could ride him, and I'll bet you I *will* ride him before the day is over. You can tell him that for me, if you will.

MRS. LEOPARD: I just can't believe I'm hearing you right.

MR. HARE *(mimicking her voice).* Oh, you're hearing me right.

(MRS. LEOPARD *looks at him, almost realizing he is mocking her.* MR. HARE *stops the mimicking and continues in his own voice.)*

Guess I'll go home again and lie down. Goodbye, Mrs. Leopard.

MRS. LEOPARD: Good-bye, Mr. Hare. *(Calling after him.)* And you'd better be more careful.

(MR. HARE *leaves slowly with his sick act until he is out of* MRS. LEOPARD*'s sight; then he skips merrily home in the reverse pattern of his trip to her house. Just before he reaches home,* MR. LEOPARD *rushes past him and exits in the direction of his own house.* MR. HARE *stops short with leg in mid-air.)*

MR. HARE *(to audience).* Leopards might be big, but they aren't very bright.
(Runs and stops short again.)

It's time they learned their lesson.
(Finishes trip home, ending with a jump in front of his house.)

I'd better get the bridle and whip ready for my ride.
(He gets stick and rope, or mimes getting them, and sits down to wait, pretending to be very unconcerned.)

MR. LEOPARD   *(rushing on in terrible anger).* Mr. Hare! Mr. Hare!

MR. HARE   *(jumping up bright and hoppity).* Greetings, Mr. Leopard. How are you?

MR. LEOPARD   *(confused).* Ah . . . Greetings. *(Refocusing his anger.)* Mr. Hare . . .

MR. HARE: I saw you several times earlier. Sorry you didn't have time to say hello.

MR. LEOPARD: I was in a hurry. *(Angrily.)* Mr. Hare . . .

MR. HARE: How are you, by the way?

MR. LEOPARD: Fine.
(Exasperated, he grabs MR. HARE *and leans on him to stop his jumping around.)*

Listen, Mr. Hare. My wife said you were by my house earlier and boasted you would ride me like a horse.

MR. HARE   *(slipping out from his grip).* Heavens, that's ridiculous, Mr. Leopard!

MR. LEOPARD: It's worse than ridiculous. It's insulting.
*(*MR. LEOPARD *paces up and down during this exchange, and* MR. HARE *mimics him, falling in with the pacing with mock sympathy.)*

MR. HARE: It is very insulting!

MR. LEOPARD: I'm absolutely furious.

MR. HARE: I would be, too!

MR. LEOPARD *(stops).* Wait, now you're the one who said that.
(MR. HARE *gives innocent shrug.)* My wife said so!

MR. HARE: Maybe your wife was mistaken.

MR. LEOPARD *(circling him and speaking slowly and deliberately).* My wife told me very clearly that you told her to give me the message that you would ride me like a horse.

MR. HARE: There must be some mistake.

MR. LEOPARD: Now, wait a minute. *(Reflects.)* My wife wouldn't just make up a story like that. There is no mistake. *(To* MR. HARE *with anger.)* And no one is going to make a fool out of me.

MR. HARE: Certainly not, Mr. Leopard.

MR. LEOPARD *(very sure of himself).* I want to hear the two of you straighten this out. Come on home with me. *(He starts to leave, assuming* MR. HARE *will follow.)* I'll ask my wife to repeat the message in front of you.

MR. HARE *(brightly).* I'd really like to come with you, Mr. Leopard *(changes instantly to sick act),* but I'm sick today. Didn't Mrs. Leopard tell you? I barely made it home myself.

MR. LEOPARD   *(exasperated).* Come on! You know I live nearby.

MR. HARE   *(collapsing).* That's true, but I'm feeling weaker every minute. I know I'd never be able to walk that far today.

MR. LEOPARD   *(furious).* I have been insulted to-day, and the matter is going to be settled today! Do you hear?

MR. HARE   *(weakly).* I don't see why it can't wait until I'm feeling stronger.

MR. LEOPARD: You're coming with me today, even if I have to carry you! *(Grabs his arm and pulls him to his feet.)*

MR. HARE   *(weakly).* All right, then. You'll have to carry me; I'm too weak to walk. *(He sinks down again.)*

MR. LEOPARD   *(thoroughly exasperated and frustrated).* Hurry up. Get on my back. *(Bends over.)*

MR. HARE   *(with a sparkle).* If you insist!
(Jumps up and runs around to get ready to mount. Almost gives in to the temptation to kick MR. LEOPARD *in the rear while mounting but resists it; then decides to have a little more fun before getting on. Leans meekly on* MR. LEOP-ARD*'s back.)*

I'm afraid I'll fall off your back while you're running. Do you mind if I get a little rope?

MR. LEOPARD *(considers and is unable to think of any objection).* Nope.

MR. HARE *(gets rope and stops in front of* MR. LEOPARD, *looking him in the eye).*
I'll just put this through your mouth so I'll have something to hang on to.
*(*MR. LEOPARD *nods, and* MR. HARE *does the business of putting rope in* MR. LEOPARD*'s mouth. Again* MR. HARE *starts to mount, is tempted to kick him, but thinks better of it; he leans on* MR. LEOPARD*'s back.)*

MR. HARE: Now I need a little stick.

MR. LEOPARD *(speaking through clenched teeth).* What for?

MR. HARE *(directly to* MR. LEOPARD*'s face).* To push aside the low branches so they won't knock me off your back while you're running.

MR. LEOPARD *(considers briefly).* Okay.
*(*MR. HARE *gets stick.)*

MR. HARE *(runs around to mount).* I'm ready now. *(He thinks of one more thing.)* Could you get a little lower?
(As MR. LEOPARD *continues to respond,* MR. HARE *skips around with increasing delight at the situation.)*

Lower, lower, lower, lower . . . *(*MR. LEOPARD *looks around at him.)*

. . . Ah, steady! *(With mock seriousness.)* Now let me get hold of the rope . . . and my stick . . . *(Jumps on* MR. LEOPARD's *back.)*

. . . We're off!
(They gallop to the LEOPARD *house along the path that* MR. HARE *previously ran. Drum can accompany this action.)*

MR. HARE: Faster, Mr. Leopard, faster. *(Using the stick.)*
*(*MRS. LEOPARD *comes out to establish the house.)*

MR. HARE   *(as they pull up in front of house).* Hello, there, Mrs. Leopard!

MR. LEOPARD   *(very authoritatively).* We just came by to check up on the boast that Mr. Hare would ride me like a horse.
*(*MRS. LEOPARD *looks alarmed as* MR. LEOPARD *slowly straightens up. It almost dawns on* MR. LEOPARD *what has happened.* MR. HARE *slowly slides off his back and steps aside.)*

MR. HARE: Well, guess I'll be going now. I feel lots better. *(Starts moving off.)*
Thanks for the ride.

MR. LEOPARD: Like a horse!
(Realization hits; he throws MRS. LEOPARD *a look and tears off, chasing* MR. HARE *with a roar. Both exit in chase.* MRS. LEOPARD *exits slowly shaking her head.)*

SECOND INTERLUDE
(optional)

Here is another place for extra music and dance. The Narrator with the help of the musicians could teach the audience rhythms to clap or songs to sing. When you invite an audience to join in, it usually works best to ask them to do a small amount at first and a little more each time they're asked. In this way, if you wish, you can work up to a point where everybody dances together at the end.

Finish the interlude on a quiet note so everyone will be ready for the beginning of the next tale.

ANANSE'S TRICK DOES DOUBLE WORK

Ananse is the trickster spider of Ashanti folklore from Ghana. This spider is so tricky that long ago, he even tricked Nyame, the sky-god, into giving him his stories, which are now known as Ananse tales. Some creatures, however, began to get wise to Ananse's ways.

CHARACTERS

ANANSE (the spider)   LION
GOAT   TURKEY
WART HOG

PROP LIST

(These things can be real or mimed.)

HAND PROPS   STAGE PROPS

bag of corn   tree
string of fish   large rock
basket of nuts

NARRATOR: Listen. Someone's coming.
(*Singing of* GOAT *and other animals is heard from off stage.*)

More than one. Let's see what they're up to. (WART HOG *enters carrying a load of corn on his back. He is slow and deliberate in his pace.* LION, *authoritative but not too bright, is right behind with a large string of fish. Silly, giddy* GOAT *comes skipping around them holding a basket of kola nuts and singing a bright little tune.*)
(ANANSE, *the spider, enters from the other side. He is lackadaisical until he spots the party; their goods interest him.*)

GOAT (*seeing the spider*).
Hey, hey there, Ananse!

ANANSE: Hello, Goat. Say, hello there, Lion. (*Pausing to show his scorn.*) Hello, Wart Hog.

WART HOG: Hello, Mr. Spider.

LION: Hello, Spiderman.

ANANSE: Off to market?

GOAT: Yes, come on with us. I'm going to sell my kola nuts.

ANANSE   *(sees them and nods).* Maybe I will. *(Looks at* LION*'s goods.)* Those are beautiful fish you have, Lion.

LION: Just caught them this morning.

ANANSE: I'll bet you've got corn in your bag, Wart Hog. *(Pokes the bag.)*

WART HOG: Right. My whole field is ripe now.

ANANSE: Well, let's go.

WART HOG: Wait a minute. Do you have anything to sell?

ANANSE: No. What does that matter? I'll just come along with all of you.

WART HOG: Oh no you don't. Now I know why you're so interested in what we have.

LION: Yes, the last time you came along, I lost everything I brought with me.

GOAT: That's right. No more of your tricks, Ananse.

WART HOG   *(to* GOAT *and* LION*).* Let's go. *(To* ANANSE.*)* I'm not going to let you trick me again. If you want some goods, you're going to have to work for them.
(The three start to leave.)

ANANSE: Work! You have to be stupid to work!
(They start back toward him protesting indignantly.)

LION *(stopping the others).* Very well. *(Decides not to take the remark personally.)* But don't expect to come with us.
(They start to leave again.)

ANANSE: There are easier ways than working. I'll use my head.

LION: You do it your way. We'll do it ours.
(Group continues on to market making a circle and exiting.)

ANANSE: That's just fine with me.
(TURKEY enters with a jerky walk from the other side and stops upon seeing ANANSE. TURKEY is wiry, alert, and nobody's fool. He must be obviously bald.)

I will do it my way, and I'll let all of you help me, too. Wait a few minutes and see if you don't.
(Runs off after others.)

TURKEY *(to the audience).* He's up to his tricks again. *(Walks a circle.)* I don't know what it is, but I'd better find the others to warn them something is up.
(He considers which direction to go and exits after ANANSE.)
(The circling group reappears and again exits. ANANSE runs on and catches LION before he disappears.)

ANANSE: Lion, Lion . . . wait!

LION *(turning back from others)*. Well, what is it now, Ananse?

ANANSE: There's something very important I have to tell you. I didn't want to say it in front of the others. But you are Lion, and you should know.

LION *(flattered)*. Yes, of course, what is it, Spider?

ANANSE: The reason I don't want to go to market alone is that I'm afraid.

LION *(scoffing)*. What is there to be afraid of?

ANANSE: Something terrible. Listen. Last night I had a dream about Old Hag.

LION *(startled and worried)*. Old Hag!

ANANSE: Shh. Yes, Old Hag. She came to me in my dream and said she is going to come and bring trouble to everyone in this district.

LION: Why?

ANANSE: Because everyone here keeps saying bad things about each other.

LION: No . . .

ANANSE: But we do. Didn't I just call all of you stupid for working?

LION: Yes.

ANANSE: You see? Old Hag is sure to get us.

LION: You're right. Oh, no!

ANANSE: Do you think we should warn the others?

LION: Of course, we should warn them.

ANANSE: They'll never listen to me.

LION: Oh, they'll listen to me. I'll call them.
    *(His call should be loud and rhythmical to begin
    the feeling of a chant for the dialogue that fol-
    lows. This next sequence builds in intensity be-
    tween leader and chorus like a revival meeting.)*

    Aye yee, aye yee, ah ooh la,
    Aye yee, aye yee . . .

WART HOG   *(hurrying on).* What is it?

LION: . . . Come and listen.

GOAT   *(hurrying on).* Quick, quick. What's the mat-
    ter?

LION: Ananse had a dream . . .

GOAT: A dream?

ANANSE: A dream about Old Hag.

GOAT and WART HOG: Oh . . . ah . . . *(They run
    about in panic.)*

ANANSE: She came to me in the dream . . .

ALL: Aye . . . *(They try to hide behind each other.)*

ANANSE: And she let out a cry, "Yah!"

ALL: Yee . . .

ANANSE: She said, "Everybody in this district talks too much about each other . . ."

ALL: Oh . . . *(Recognition of the truth.)*

ANANSE: ". . . says bad things about each other."

ALL: Yes, yes.

ANANSE: She said, "If this does not stop . . ."

ALL *(on an in-breath)*. Hah. Yes.
(Holding to listen.)

ANANSE: "If it does not stop, Ananse, I will come to you . . ."

ALL: Ah . . .

ANANSE: ". . . I will find out who it is . . ."

ALL *(higher pitch)*. Ah . . .

ANANSE: ". . . and I will bring trouble for everyone!"
(All start a loud wailing and dashing about. TURKEY *enters with his staccato walk.)*

TURKEY: What is it? Why are you wailing?

GOAT *(running by him)*. She's coming.

LION: Old Hag is coming.

WART HOG: Coming to bring trouble to the district.

60

(All continue to wail and run about, and TUR-
KEY, *whipped up into the frenzy, joins them.)*

TURKEY *(collecting himself)*. Stop. Can't we do
something?
(Others stop and look.)

Can't we do something?
(They all look around and end up focusing on
LION.*)*

LION *(rising to the occasion with pompous authority)*. Yes, yes. Certainly we can do something.
(Pause.)

ANANSE *(prompting* LION*)*. Stop talking about each
other.

LION: We can all stop talking about each other. Do
you understand?

TURKEY *(realizes from hearing* ANANSE *prompt*
LION *that this might be part of a trick)*. Wait a
minute. Something's fishy. And I just overheard
Ananse . . .

LION *(stops him pompously)*. Do not let Old Hag
hear you say one bad thing about each other
ever again.

TURKEY: But . . .

LION: Now everybody go about his business!

ANANSE: Shhh!

WART HOG: We'll be very careful. *(Walking by* ANANSE.) Shhh. *(Exits.)*

GOAT: Not a word. *(Walks by* ANANSE, *returning the Shhh. Exits in same direction.)*
(LION exits with the same Shhh. TURKEY *starts to say something again, but* ANANSE *catches his eye and gives a strong Shhh.* TURKEY *decides not to argue. Shrugs. Starts to walk off in other direction, stops.)*

TURKEY *(to the audience).* Hope it works. *(Exits.)*

ANANSE: It will work . . . for me! Good start. Those sillies are really scared. Let's see. *(Notices a rock under his foot. Rock can be mimed.)* This rock should work. I'm ready.
(WART HOG re-enters and ANANSE leaps up and starts to move the rock.)

WART HOG *(still carrying load of corn).* I don't think I'll go to market today. I'm not really scared. But it doesn't seem like a good day to go. *(ANANSE is struggling with rock, grunting loudly.* WART HOG notices him, stops. Silence. ANANSE starts up again. WART HOG looks back at him.)*

Oh, Ananse, what are you doing?

ANANSE: Moving this rock.

WART HOG *(nods).* Why are you moving it, Ananse?

ANANSE: I decided you were right, Wart Hog, about working. It would be nice to have some corn. I'm going to raise some. I just have to get this rock over a little farther.

WART HOG: Good for you. *(Watches a moment.)* Why are you moving the rock, Ananse?

ANANSE: Careful, don't step there! That's where I've planted the corn. Can you give me a hand with this rock?

WART HOG: I'll be glad to help. Let me put down my corn. *(He puts it down, and they start to move the rock together.)* I've had experience raising corn all my life.

ANANSE: Yes, I know. Over this way a little more. *(They struggle.)* A little more. Good. *(They lower the rock.)*

WART HOG: Ananse, you just said you planted corn on this spot.

ANANSE: Right.

WART HOG: And you want it to grow?

ANANSE: Of course.

WART HOG: And you put a rock on top of it?

ANANSE: Certainly. I don't want anyone to step on it.

WART HOG: That's the dumbest thing I've ever heard.

ANANSE: What?

WART HOG: You're stupid!

ANANSE: Shhh. Oh, no. Old Hag will get you.

WART HOG: Oh! What did I say! Please don't let her know. Don't tell her.

ANANSE: She probably already heard.

WART HOG: I didn't mean to say it. Please help me.

ANANSE: She'll be pretty mad. Maybe you could give her something.

WART HOG: Yes, yes. I'll give her something. *(Pacing around.)* Something, something, something. *(Pause.)* What?

ANANSE: Hmmm. . . . Your corn?

WART HOG: Yes! I'll give you some corn to give her.

ANANSE: Of course, I'm very busy right now with this corn that I'm raising.

WART HOG: Ananse, listen. You can have the rest of it for yourself. Here's the whole load.

ANANSE: Well, all right. Since you're an old friend, I'll help you out. Give it to me.

WART HOG: Oh, thank you so much, Ananse. I'm

64

going home. I can't make it to market today. I'm just not up to it.

ANANSE: Good-bye, Wart Hog.

WART HOG: Thanks very much, Ananse.

ANANSE: Don't mention it.
(WART HOG *exits.*)

Don't mention it to a soul. *(Laughs.)* That was the easiest way to get corn that I ever saw! *(Sits down with corn, hears* LION *approaching, and jumps up to work with rock.)*

LION *(walking thoughtfully home with his string of fish).* Humph. Humph.
(ANANSE *struggles and grunts with rock, trying to pick it up.)*

Why, Ananse, what are you doing here? (ANANSE *continues his struggle.)* Ananse!

ANANSE: Oh, I didn't notice you, Lion. You're just the one I want to see. I'm going fishing. Would you give me a hand with this?

LION: Well, certainly, but both my hands are tied up right now with my own load of fish.

ANANSE: Could you put it down for a minute and give me a hand?

LION: Yes, of course, I could. *(He puts fish down.)* Here, let me give you a hand with that rock.

ANANSE: Yes, thank you.
　　(Rock is in his arms.)

　　Help me get it on my shoulder.
　　(LION *tries to help but is actually useless.)*

　　If you get under it and let me turn around . . .

LION: Yes, I was just going to say, if I get under it,
　　then you can turn around . . .

ANANSE: And we'll get it on my shoulder.

LION: Yes, right on your shoulder. *(Helps to do this.)*

ANANSE: That's good. Thanks a lot, friend. Now wish
　　me luck.

LION: Why wish you luck?

ANANSE: Because I'm off to go fishing. I hope to
　　catch a lot.

LION: Wait a minute! If you're off to go fishing, why
　　are you taking that rock?

ANANSE: I need the rock to catch the fish.

LION: Catch fish with a rock?

ANANSE: Yes.

LION: No one ever fishes with a rock!

ANANSE: That's the point! No one ever uses a rock,
　　so the fish won't expect it. I'll fool them.

LION: Impossible.

ANANSE *(mimes as he talks)*. I'll sneak up to the edge of the water . . .

LION: Ananse, you need a fish hook . . .

ANANSE: . . . and I'll watch for one to swim by . . .

LION: . . . or a fish net.

ANANSE: . . . and then I'll pretend to look the other way . . .

LION: Listen to me! I know how to do it!

ANANSE: . . . and I'll drop this rock on his head! *(Drops it.)*

Crrrash!

LION: That will never work, you fool!

ANANSE: What!

LION: You're a fool. A stupid, stubborn fool!

ANANSE: Oh no . . .
(Claps his hand over LION*'s mouth.)*

Old Hag!

LION: Old Hag!

ANANSE: Why did you say that! Now she'll come and bring trouble.

LION: What have I done! Don't tell her. Ananse, do not tell her!

ANANSE: She's going to ask.

LION: Please help me, friend.

ANANSE: Maybe you could give her something.

LION: Of course, of course. That's what I'll do. *(Pause.)* But I don't have anything.

ANANSE: What about these fish?

LION: Of course, please give her a fish.

ANANSE: Well, it's a risk for me.

LION: Here, take the rest for yourself.

ANANSE: All right. Since you are Lion, I'll do you a favor.

LION: Thank you, Ananse.

ANANSE: Don't mention it.

LION: No, I certainly won't.

ANANSE: Good-bye, Lion. Glad I could help. *(*LION *exits.)* One drop of the rock caught a whole load of fish! Come on, over here with the corn. Now I'll find a big basket to carry everything to market.
*(*GOAT *is heard singing off stage.)*

Oh, first Goat!
(Returns to work on rock.)

GOAT *(nervously tripping on stage without the nuts).* Oh, Ananse. Am I glad to find someone!

68

Have you seen Wart Hog? Have you seen Turkey?
(Willing to find anyone.) Have you seen Lion?

ANANSE: I can't talk now. I'm busy.

GOAT: Oh, yes, of course. Don't let me bother you.
(ANANSE still struggles with rock.)

What are you doing, Ananse?

ANANSE: Getting kola nuts.

GOAT: You're getting nuts from that rock? *(Giggles
at his own joke.)*

ANANSE: Of course not. I'm going to get them from
that tree you're standing under.

GOAT   *(looking up).* Oh, yes. You're going to stand on
the rock to climb the tree.

ANANSE: Look out.
(GOAT watches intently.)

One, two, three!
*(ANANSE throws rock into tree; rock falls with a
thud. A drum can make the sound if the rock is
mimed.)*

GOAT: Ananse, what are you doing?

ANANSE: I'm going to knock those nuts out of the
tree.

GOAT   *(giggling).* But, Ananse, you have to climb the
tree so you can pick them or shake them down.

ANANSE: I just have to throw this rock a little higher. Look out! *(Holds rock over his head.)*

GOAT: You'd better climb that tree.

ANANSE: This is easier.
(Throws rock again, and it falls with a thud.)

GOAT: You think it is easier to take this great big rock and stand under this great big tree and try to hit that little tiny nut way up there?

ANANSE: Maybe if I ran first. *(Struggles to pick up rock, runs, throws it; it lands with a thud.)*

GOAT: I used to think I was silly. *(Giggles.)*

ANANSE: I think I have to run faster.
(Tries again.)

GOAT: This is the silliest thing I've ever seen.

ANANSE: Once more. *(Starts to pick up rock.)*

GOAT: Ananse, you are crazy. *(Giggling.)*

ANANSE   *(drops rock at his feet).* What?

GOAT   *(giggling).* Crazy, crazy, crazy.

ANANSE: Old Hag!

GOAT: Oh, no. Oh!

ANANSE: I'm sorry you said that, Goat.

GOAT: Oh, help.

ANANSE: All right. What will you do for me?

GOAT: What *can* I do for you?

ANANSE: Give me your kola nuts. Where are they?

GOAT: I hid them back on the road.

ANANSE: Go get them and leave them here with my other things. I have to run home for a basket. I'm in a hurry.
(GOAT *runs off.*)

What a load of goods I'll have! The basket. *(Exits in another direction.)*
(TURKEY picks his way on stage, entering from a third area. GOAT comes tearing on with his basket of nuts and runs into TURKEY.)

TURKEY: Say, Goat. Where are you going so fast with those nuts?

GOAT   *(skittering around to put them with the pile of goods).* Quick, I have to give these kola nuts to Ananse.

TURKEY: But Ananse isn't here.

GOAT: That's all right. He said to just leave them with his other things.

LION   *(entering).* Where's Ananse? He was supposed to do me a favor.

TURKEY: Ananse isn't here.

GOAT: But his goods are. Here's the pile.

TURKEY: Wait a minute. How could Ananse suddenly have a pile of goods?
(WART HOG enters.)

He didn't have anything this morning.

LION: Yeh!

GOAT: Yeh!

LION   *(turns on GOAT).* How did he get them?

GOAT   *(jumping).* I don't know. I just came with my kola nuts, and all these other things were here.

WART HOG: I gave him my load of corn, but I don't know how he got the other things.

LION: The only thing I know about is the string of fish I gave him.

TURKEY: But that's all there is: fish, corn, and nuts. The things all came from you.

ALL   *(simultaneously to each other).* Why did you . . .

GOAT: Old Hag.

WART HOG: Yes, to give to Old Hag.

LION: So she won't hurt us.

TURKEY: But why give the things to Ananse?

LION: Ananse is the one who saw Old Hag.

72

TURKEY: Wait. *(Shakes head.)* You gave your goods to Ananse to give to Old Hag? *(All nod.)* And Ananse is the only one who has heard from Old Hag?

GOAT: He dreamed about her.

TURKEY: He dreamed her up, if you ask me!

ALL: Oh, no. *(Talking over each other's words.)* He tricked us! What a cheat! Let me take my things back.

TURKEY *(silencing them).* Wait. Don't take them back. Let's make Ananse give them back.

ALL: How?

TURKEY: I know Ananse. Let me do it. Here he comes! Go hide in the bushes.
(Group hides and TURKEY *sneaks out unseen by* ANANSE *who runs on, jumping over rock.)*

ANANSE: I couldn't find a basket anywhere. I'll just have to carry my things without one.
(He starts gathering up his goods, TURKEY *enters, struts along, walking carefully around the rock.* ANANSE *sees him.)*

Oh, Turkey!
*(*ANANSE *runs over to his rock and starts to pick it up again.* TURKEY *walks by indifferently, preening himself.* ANANSE *grunts and puffs. No reaction from* TURKEY. ANANSE *picks up rock*

and drops it to make large noise. TURKEY *stops but then makes a point of noticing something else other than the crash.* ANANSE *picks up rock and starts to move after* TURKEY. TURKEY *pretends to have forgotten something and starts to walk back, passing* ANANSE *who's holding the rock.* ANANSE *drops rock behind* TURKEY *on path.* TURKEY *stops, as though realizing he doesn't need the forgotten thing anyway, and returns. He trips over rock and continues without noticing either it or* ANANSE. *For extra emphasis* NARRATOR *can accompany* TURKEY'*s jerky, deliberate walk with tapping or plucking sounds, such as those made on a wood block, thumb piano, or taut string over cigar box.)*

ANANSE   *(unable to contain himself any longer).* Turkey! Turkey!

TURKEY   *(stops).* Oh, hello there, Ananse. I didn't notice you. *(Continues walking.)*

ANANSE: Where are you going?

TURKEY: Into town.

ANANSE: I'm trying to manage this rock.

TURKEY: Um hum. Well, see you later. *(Continues to leave.)*

ANANSE: Wait. Could you help me with this rock?

TURKEY: Well, I'm going to town right now.

74

ANANSE: Why the hurry?

TURKEY *(coming back to circle* ANANSE*).* To get a hair cut.

ANANSE: To get a hair cut?

TURKEY: Um hum.

ANANSE: You haven't got any hair.

TURKEY: Maybe some will grow if I have a hair cut.

ANANSE: That will never work. Who ever heard of such a thing!

TURKEY: It's worth a try.

ANANSE *(laughing).* Oh, you are crazy.

TURKEY: What?

ANANSE: Absolutely crazy!

TURKEY: Old Hag, Ananse!

ANANSE *(so caught up in his own story that now he believes it).* Oh, no!

TURKEY: She'll get you!

ANANSE *(frantic).* Please don't tell her.

TURKEY: What can I do?

ANANSE: Oh, help!

TURKEY: Maybe you could give her something.

ANANSE: Yes, yes. I'd better give her something. *(Pause.)* But I don't have a single thing to give.

TURKEY *(Pointing to the pile of goods).* What about all these things?

ANANSE: Oh, yes, I guess I could give her some of this.

TURKEY: She's going to be mad.

ANANSE: I'll give her everything!

TURKEY: Here she comes now!
(LION, WART HOG, *and* GOAT *come out from hiding. Clinging together, they form a monster–like figure, waving their arms and roaring.)*

ANANSE *(dashes behind* TURKEY *keeping his back to "Old Hag.")* Don't hurt me! I'll give you everything, Old Hag.

TURKEY: Old Hag is waiting, Ananse.

ANANSE: Old Hag, please let me give you this corn and fish and . . .
(He turns around quickly and sees the three.)

   . . . nuts!

LION: I'll let you give it to me, Ananse.

WART HOG: Right here, Ananse.

GOAT *(giggling).* If you insist, I'll take my nuts.
(Each takes his goods.)

76

LION *(to all but* ANANSE*).* Come on. Let's go to market.

(*All dance off.* ANANSE *is furious at having lost this round. He stomps off in other direction.* TURKEY *looks after him, laughs, stops, looks at audience, and gives ruffling shake to his tail feathers. Exits in a third direction.*)

THIRD INTERLUDE
(optional)

As you change the scenery after the Ananse play, remember to clear away the rock, even if it's an imaginary one!

If you've already had the audience sing or clap along with your drumming and music, you might now teach them to chant some words in an African language. For instance, one, two, three, four in Swahili is *moja* (móh jah), *mbili* (m bée lee), *tatu* (taĥ tu), *nne* (ń neh). And *"Jambo, habari gani?"* (jaĥm boh, hah bah ree ǵah nee) means "Hello, what news?" or "Hello, what's happening?" If you want to use more African words and expressions, ask someone who speaks one of the many African languages to teach you, so you can be sure of correct usage and pronunciation.

This interlude needs to end on a quiet note so that the musicians and Narrator can create a gentle feeling for the beginning of the next play.

THE TURTLE WHO WANTED TO FLY

Turtles often appear in tales of the Yoruba people of Nigeria. Parts of this tale also came from a Jamaican Ananse or Nancy tale.

CHARACTERS

TURTLE	FARMER
PIGEON 1	BOY
PIGEON 2	WIFE

PROP LIST

(These things can be real or mimed.)

HAND PROPS

feathers that can be
    pulled off Pigeons and
    stuck onto Turtle
rope
corn

(The mood of this play is soft, lyrical, and whim-sical. It might be established with the sound of orchestra bells, water glasses, xylophone, marimba, or flute. The instrument you choose could then be used to accompany TURTLE's sing-ing.)

NARRATOR: There was once a turtle who was a dreamer. He couldn't run very fast. And he couldn't swim very far. He couldn't dance very well. But he could sing just beautifully.
(TURTLE enters singing a la-de-da tune without words.)

NARRATOR: And because he could sing very well, he would sing for hours every day. Sometimes he would sing about things he liked.
(TURTLE sings to himself a little song without words that deals with things he likes.)

NARRATOR: And sometimes he would sing about things he didn't like.
(TURTLE sings a little wordless song about hate-ful things.)

NARRATOR: But mostly he would sing about things he wished he could do.

TURTLE   (while singing, he attempts to do these actions).
I wish I could swim like a wiley green crocodile.
I wish I could run like a lovely gazelle.
I wish I could swing from my tail like a monkey,
And, if I try hard enough,
And, if I try hard enough,
And, if I try hard enough,
   you never can tell,
   you never can tell,
If I try hard enough,
   perhaps I could do it!

NARRATOR: But what he really wanted to do more than anything else was to fly.
(PIGEONS fly in a circle around the stage. Actors can make up any movement they wish for the flying. TURTLE stops singing and watches them in awe.)

TURTLE: Oh, I wish I could fly. I wish I could fly more than anything else in the world. If I could take up flying, I'd even give up singing. Yes, gladly.
(PIGEONS fly by again.)

TURTLE: Birds! Say, Pigeons! Please come here. I want to talk to you, but I can't go that fast.

PIGEON 1:   Hello there, Turtle. (Landing).

PIGEON 2:   (landing). Hello, friend. We thought we heard you singing as we flew by.

82

PIGEON 1: It sounded lovely. It makes me feel like flying.

PIGEON 2: Would you mind singing another little tune right now? I'd like to try it out.

TURTLE: Yes, I'll sing a verse or two. *(He sings his little tune.)*
(PIGEONS are taken over by the song and dance-fly until TURTLE stops singing.)

PIGEON 1 *(landing beside TURTLE)*. That was marvelous.

PIGEON 2 *(landing)*. When you sing, it makes me feel like dancing-flying.

TURTLE: Oh, thank you. It makes me feel like flying, too. In fact I always feel like flying. But I can't. I've tried and tried, but I absolutely can't do it. Would you watch me? Maybe you can tell what I'm doing wrong.
(PIGEONS watch while TURTLE makes a very concentrated and clumsy attempt to move his flippers and feet; his shell restricts him severely.)

PIGEON 1: You are trying hard enough . . .

PIGEON 2: . . . But it will never work. If you ask me, it's because you have no feathers.

PIGEON 1: Feathers! Why, last year, when I moulted and lost all my feathers . . .

PIGEON 2: . . . you couldn't fly a bit.

PIGEON 1: Right. I had to wait till they'd all grown in again.

TURTLE: Feathers! I've never had any feathers. I don't think I'll ever grow any either, because I've been waiting to fly for a long time and not a single feather has grown.

PIGEON 2: Look, I'll give you a few of mine. I don't need *every* last one.

PIGEON 1: I can spare some, too. I'd like to help you out with this because I certainly do appreciate your singing for us.
(PIGEONS *take feathers from their wings and stick them in the* TURTLE'*s shell.*)

TURTLE (*growing more and more excited as each feather is added*). I'm beautiful! Oh, look, how beautiful I am!
(*He spins around to display feathers.*)

I feel all dressed up with no place to go. Where shall we fly?

PIGEON 1: We were just on our way to the corn field over there next to you. Come along with us, and we'll have a corn feast to celebrate.
(PIGEONS *fly to the far side of stage, and* TURTLE *follows clumsily, but too excited to notice his "flying" doesn't work very well.*)

TURTLE: This is wonderful. I am flying! I am just like one of the pigeons.

PIGEON 1:   The corn is much better than it was last week.

PIGEON 2:   It's not bad. Fuller kernels. *(To* TURTLE.*)* Are you enjoying it, friend?

TURTLE: Oh . . . yes, delicious experience. *(He tries to eat with the rest of them but is too excited.)*

PIGEON 1:   I was afraid it would never ripen.

PIGEON 2:   Well, there wasn't enough sun for it until this week.

PIGEON 1:   True. *(To* TURTLE.*)* Say, don't eat the husk. The good part's inside.

TURTLE   *(in confused manner).* Yes, of course. I'm getting to it now.

PIGEON 1   *(moving to a new place for more corn, notices something off stage).*
Quick! Fly. The farmer's coming.

PIGEON 2   *(darting over to look).* His boy is with him, too. Get out fast.

PIGEON 1:   They killed two crows last week. Hurry up.
(The PIGEONS *fly around the* TURTLE *with great alarm.* PIGEON 1 *exits one way.)*

PIGEON 2: Come on! Fly. Fly. *(Exits another way.)*

TURTLE: I'm coming. Don't wait. I can't fly as fast as you can yet. I'll catch up in a minute.
(TURTLE tries to fly, flapping his flippers fiercely. He covers no ground. FARMER and BOY enter, see him; FARMER signals to BOY to grab TURTLE. FARMER is overly authoritative in his commands, and the BOY is so full of fun and the silliness of things that the FARMER's commands don't get through to him.)

FARMER: Get him.
(They do a slapstick mix-up here with BOY grabbing FARMER, who then throws him off. Each grabs for a flipper, but TURTLE quickly pulls flippers into his shell. FARMER finally seizes TURTLE by neck.)

FARMER: I've got him. Go get a rope.

BOY: Rope? *(Playing with the sounds of the word.)* Rope, rope, rope . . .

FARMER: The rope!
(BOY dashes off to get it.)

We can have stewed turtle with our corn tonight.
(BOY dashes back on immediately with rope.

TURTLE: I'm not a turtle. I'm a bird.

FARMER: You look like a turtle to me. *(They put rope around his neck.)*

TURTLE: Well, I'm a flying turtle.

BOY: Then, why didn't you fly?

TURTLE *(hurt by the truth)*. Oh . . .
(FARMER *and* BOY *start to walk home with the* TURTLE *between them.)*

NARRATOR: Yes, the turtle was disappointed. But he realized this was no time for wishful thinking, so he said to himself:

TURTLE: Under the circumstances, I think I'd better give up flying and take up singing.
(TURTLE *starts to sing and* FARMER *and* BOY, *overcome by the sound, begin to sway and dance, increasing their movements until they completely entangle themselves and the* TURTLE *with rope.* TURTLE *stops singing.)*

FARMER: Now, look what you've done!

BOY: It wasn't my fault. You were dancing, too.

FARMER: Never mind about that. Get me untangled.
(BOY *makes it worse.)*

No, the other way.
(They get straightened out.)

I'll take the turtle home; you get the corn.

BOY: Corn?
(Again playing with the sounds of the word.)

Corn, corn, corn . . .

FARMER: Go get the corn!

BOY: Corn! *(Dashes out and falls down before disappearing, off stage.)*
(FARMER starts to walk home with TURTLE on rope. BOY appears again and mischievously slaps out a rhythm on his leg.)

FARMER: The corn! *(BOY scrambles out again.)*
(FARMER continues walk home. WIFE comes out to establish the house.)

FARMER: Wife, here is a surprise for you. We caught a delicious turtle for supper. Start to cook him . . .

TURTLE: Oh! *(Shrinks into shell. FARMER and WIFE look with surprise.)*

FARMER: . . . while I go help our boy get the corn.

WIFE: Gladly. This is a treat. He'll be ready to eat by the time you get back. *(FARMER leaves and WIFE prepares to go to work.)*

(Looks TURTLE over carefully, becoming puzzled). What a strange looking creature you are, covered with feathers. Shall I cook you like a bird or like a turtle?

NARRATOR: The turtle felt he had really nothing to lose at this point, so he spoke up:

TURTLE: I think I'm better as a turtle. You could pluck off my feathers, and I'll look exactly like a turtle again.

WIFE: Thank you for your suggestion. It's a good idea.
(She starts to remove his feathers.)

You're a very helpful sort of fellow.

NARRATOR: As the feathers were removed, the turtle began to feel like his old self again. This cheered him up a lot, and he began to sing softly. (TURTLE *begins to sing.)* Can you guess what happened this time?
(The WIFE *is taken over by* TURTLE*'s singing which gets louder and louder and she begins to dance.)*

NARRATOR: When the turtle saw what was happening, he sang all the louder. He sang and sang. The farmer returned and said:

FARMER *(enters followed by* BOY *with corn).* Why, that turtle isn't ready! What is this dancing here?
(He tries to stop his WIFE, *but he is also overcome by* TURTLE*'s singing and joins in dancing, as does the* BOY.*)*

NARRATOR: But the turtle kept on singing, and the farmer and his family danced and danced, and they never even noticed the turtle's friend come in to find him.

PIGEON 1   *(flies on).* Come on quickly. *(Motions to*
   TURTLE.) Follow me.
   (Still singing, the TURTLE *happily scutters off*
   after PIGEON *who leads him in a little path to*
   exit.)

NARRATOR: And the turtle sang very loudly and
   walked very quietly until he was out of sight.
   (FARMER, WIFE and BOY *dance off in other di-*
   rection.)

FINALE

(optional)

   The Narrator and musicians immediately
change the mood with a fast, strong drum beat for the
Finale. It can be a short, lively dance with all the performers joining in to make a colorful splash for the
closing. If you invite the audience to participate, the
dance, of course, will go on much longer and become
a party-like celebration!

ACTING IT OUT

A script gives you the words the characters are saying, but it gives only brief descriptions about where the characters are, how they look or feel, and what they're doing. As you read a script, your mind zips along filling in these details. You don't have to try to do this; your mind just does it naturally. The things that pop into your mind are what you want to be able to show with your body when you act out a play.

Read through the script several times to become familiar with what happens and how it happens, as well as with the mood and rhythm of the play. Check the script for all the things it tells you about the characters: the words they say, the things other characters say to them, or about them, and the stage directions. Some questions you might ask are: Who is he or she? What does she want? How does he feel about himself, about others, about what others are doing, about how others are treating him, about what he is doing? For instance, when the Wife in *The Man Who Loved to Laugh* sweeps the floor, is she doing it to please herself, to please her husband, to keep the house as nice as possible, or all three? When the Turtle sings a song, ask yourself, why is Turtle doing this? Is it to express some anger, to daydream, to please someone, to remind him of happy times? To find the answers, put yourself in the character's place or think of someone you know who is like the character. The answers to these questions will

91

help you know how the character moves and talks, what kinds of habits he has, how he behaves when he's by himself, or when he's with others. No one just sings a song or runs around or sweeps the floor. There are reasons; sometimes they're simple and sometimes they're complicated. The challenge and fun in the actor's job is to find these reasons and to make them clear through the way you act.

Work with a character until it feels like a real person to you and you can behave naturally as that person in any situation. To do this you can try out more than one way of playing the character. Also try miming the character using your body to express what you know about him. Change parts. Make up new situations for your character to be in. Take the situations in the script but improvise your own dialogue. Although any character you create is different from you, to some extent, it really *is* you. This is because you are using parts of yourself to bring the character alive. In other words, the character is *you,* pretending to be that certain person or animal.

You may find yourself playing a character who is very different from you or one you would hate to be in your real life, or one you'd love to be but know you probably never will be. This is part of the fun, too: having a chance to see how it feels to adopt someone else's point of view and behavior. But whether the character is different or similar to you, part of your own self must always be there or the character won't feel real to you, the other actors, or the audience.

DANCES AND MIME

DANCES

To make up dances for your character, start with the feeling the character has. Is it sorrow expressed in a mourning dance? Is it the prancing glee of a trickster? Let your body respond to the feeling, and, as you move, notice the kind of rhythm you use and the movements your body makes. Then select and repeat these patterns to make your dance.

Another way is to use the action that your character would naturally be doing, such as the Man's work in the field or the Pigeon's flying. Then stylize this realistic movement. To stylize, select a part of the movement that seems especially important and typical of the character's action. Make it clear and sharp by exaggeration, or repetition—eliminating all minor movement. By the time you add music, you have a dance.

The dances for the opening and the finale will be easier because characterization is not as important. You are simply moving to music. If you want to create the feeling of African dance, listen to records of African music. Notice the way the beats tend to take your body down into the ground. As you let the weight go down, you'll find the energy comes back up from the earth into your body. It's a different feeling than the one you get when you move to European or Asian music. The more you are able to let your body respond to the music, the easier it will be to find movements for your dances. In fact, as you listen, you'll find it hard to hold still!

Looking at African sculpture will also give you ideas, as will photographs and movies of African people dancing. You may have an opportunity to see performances by touring dance groups from Africa or there may be someone in your community who knows African dance and can give you some guidance.

MIME

Mime is movement that imitates real life actions. In a "mime show" or "pantomime," the actors are silent and communicate through action alone. These movements can be done realistically or in a stylized way. An actor can mime or pretend to be something other than a person, such as a tree or an animal. He can also mime or pretend to use something that isn't really there, such as an imaginary broom or an imaginary rock. In these cases an actor can use mime along with dialogue.

It's a challenge to be able to make imaginary things come alive. Mime can give you special effects that would be very difficult to achieve with real objects. For example, with mime you can have a really huge rock for Ananse to throw or some ears of corn that conveniently disappear as the Pigeons eat them. If you mime the use of an object, practice with the real thing to become familiar with the natural way of handling it. If you decide to exaggerate the size of your object, it's important to start with the actual size so that your exaggeration is an accurate extreme of the way you would naturally use it.

If you mime becoming an object or an animal, observe the real thing if possible. Films and pictures help if live animals or the real objects aren't available. Look for the main characteristics that create the feeling of that object or animal and let your body focus on those particular ways of moving. The animal characters in these plays really think, feel, and behave a lot like humans. Part of the fun of the stories is seeing yourself in the "what if" situation of being an animal. (It's not unlike saying to yourself, "I feel like a snapping turtle today." Or looking at a person and thinking, "He looks like a hound dog." Or, "She acts like a rhinoceros!") So you might play the animal characters very much like people with a hint of the animal or like animals with a touch of the human.

If you turn the plays into a mime show, work to make the character's actions very clear so the story can be understood through the movements alone. The movements in a mime show can be done realistically, or you may find it fun to stylize all of them so your play looks almost like a dance.

MUSIC

You may want to add music to these plays. It can help set the mood for a scene or help one play flow smoothly into the next. It can be used for emphasis when the characters are doing things, or to accompany dancing or singing.

Records are a good place to start (see the discography on page 127.) Experiment with the selections you've picked, deciding what will be the most effective and suitable for the action of the play. Try playing your own instruments along with the records. If you like to make music, of course, it's more fun to play all of it yourself. If you have an instrument that you know how to play, that's fine. But you don't have to have ready-made instruments. You can make music on things you collect or find. Here's a list of different things you might use.

INSTRUMENTS FOR PERCUSSION

SHARP SOUNDS

BEATERS

wood blocks	fingers
clavés	palms
sticks (hard wood)	sticks
stones	mallets
bones (hard and dry)	metal rods

96

DRUMMING

drums (try to get several of different pitches)
wastebaskets
kitchen pans
large tin cans
barrels
table tops
boxes (wooden or cardboard)
coffee cans with plastic tops

SHAKING SOUNDS

maracas
gourds (with pebbles or sand)
tin cans (with pebbles or sand)
plastic margarine containers (filled with rice or dried beans)
paper bags (filled with pebbles or sand)
sea shells (strung)
nuts (strung)

BODY SOUNDS

clap ⎫
slap ⎬ fingers and hands
snap ⎭

stamp ⎫
tap ⎭ feet

pop ⎫
click ⎬ tongue
cluck ⎭

RINGING SOUNDS

bells
triangles
cymbals
scrap iron
pipes
large bolts
water glasses and jars
(strike *very* lightly)

INSTRUMENTS FOR MELODIES

VOICE

singing
chanting
humming
whistling

STRUCK INSTRUMENTS

xylophones
marimbas
bells (of different pitches)
boards, sticks, or metal (cut in different lengths and suspended)
glasses and jars (filled with water to different levels)
clay flower pots (suspended on knotted ropes)

STRING INSTRUMENTS

taut strings over a cigar box
guitars
mandolins
banjos
washtub bass

WIND INSTRUMENTS

whistles
kazoos
harmonicas
recorders
flutes (wooden, bamboo, metal)

CREATING THE MUSIC

Listen to African music. As you listen, let your body sense the feeling of the rhythms and melodies. It's different from our American jazz, rock, and rhythm

98

and blues, even though they have roots in African music. The complicated rhythms are made by combining different individual rhythms. These layers of rhythm are what you want to work for. To start, however, you don't need to do complicated things. You can get very good effects by just combining simple beats and sounds.

Pick a section of the play where you know you'll want music. Decide what feeling you want the music to have. Will the music accompany a happy welcoming dance, a mourning dance, or Mr. Hare's ride on Mr. Leopard? Start an even beat or a pulse that feels right for the action. Now you have a steady tick tick. But this pulse alone can become monotonous, so build or improvise a rhythm around it. Rhythm is the repeating pattern of sounds around a steady pulse or beat. It makes the beat interesting to listen to. It has accents and silences. The rhythm can make you hear the tick tick in two's or four's or three's. There's a difference in the feeling. Try it out.

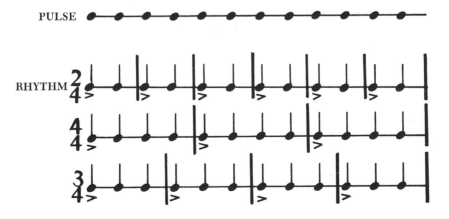

99

This main rhythm which you've established is played by a lead drummer on a strong drum, usually of medium pitch, that can be easily heard by everyone. It is up to the lead drummer to indicate to the whole group when the rhythm will change. Everyone else follows his lead and plays variations on his main rhythm.

Once you have the main rhythm established, you are ready to add other voices. In African drumming, one musician often plays a high clear bell in a rhythm that makes the main pulse very clear. This high clear sound is easy to hear and helps keep everyone together as the individual parts are added. The African bell is a piece of solid metal which is struck with a separate metal beater. Any two pieces of resonant metal will do if you don't have a bell.

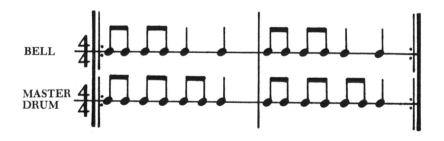

Now try adding a deep bass drum, and a high treble drum. For additional emphasis and contrast, shakers, rattles, voices, body sounds (clapping, slapping, etc.) can all be added to the main rhythm.

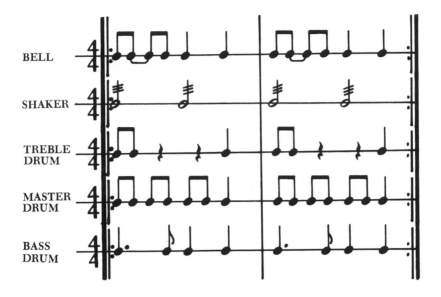

If you'd like to make the sound even more complicated, try putting together rhythms with different pulses—two's against three's, for example. The downbeat of the separate rhythms does not have to come together in African music. Learning how to keep together without having everyone use the same pulse can be very difficult, but this might be a challenge you'd like to work with. Your final combination of sounds can be as simple or as complicated as you wish to make it. Just be sure that the lead rhythm is the strongest one. Even if the musicians are not using the same downbeat, everyone must relate and listen to the main pulse, and let the leader really lead.

After you've tried out various rhythms pick the ones you like best. Think about the over-all effect you

101

want. Does the amount of sound and the kind of sound you're using feel balanced for the whole presentation? You may need to rearrange. You may have to leave out some things that are terrific by themselves but don't work with the rest of the music.

Two Ways of Playing Two's Against Threes:

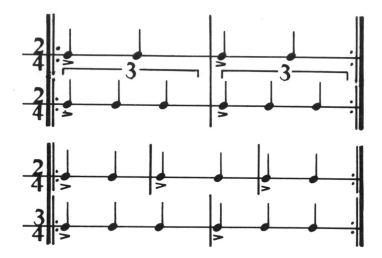

COORDINATING THE MUSIC
WITH THE ACTION

When people are going to dance to the music, play the beat at a tempo that feels comfortable for everyone. Adjust the tempo if it's too fast or too slow. The musicians need to practice playing a steady beat while they watch the performers. And the performers need to practice keeping together with the music.

There are places where music can enhance an actor's movements—when the Man does his walk-about for example, or when Turkey struts around Ananse's rock. There are also places where music can create an atmosphere or a pace that the actors can use and develop, such as when Mr. Leopard dashes past Mr. Hare's house or when the Pigeons fly about.

Music can also be used for special sound effects, helping the audience imagine what is happening. A single loud drum beat, coinciding with Ananse's large rock hitting the ground, can heighten and dramatize the moment. It helps the audience see the rock, if a real rock isn't used.

In all cases, the sound effects and the music must be coordinated with the sounds and movements of the actors. They can be coordinated through a common pulse or through the quality of a common mood or through exact timing. When everything comes together, the effect can be very exciting!

Additional Percussion Suggestions

VERY FAST

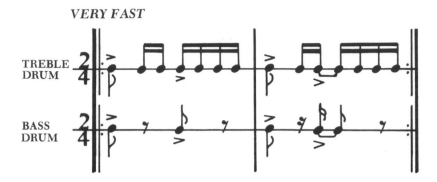

MODERATE

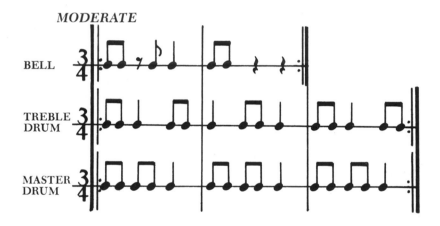

FAST

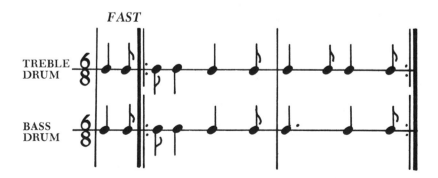

Mourning Song for *The Man Who Loved to Laugh*

(translation from Yoruba: Death is bitter; death
has taken away a good person.)

Finale Song

(words have no meaning)

SCENERY, COSTUMES, AND MASKS

SCENERY

The first question to ask about scenery is whether or not the actors need additional help in making the action and setting convincing for the audience. Do you need things to sit on, stand on, hide behind, enter from? Are you inside a house; in a field? While you may enjoy making real scenery and want the excitement of the picture that it can create for the audience, you can do all of these things through mime or pantomime. In the plays in this book characters move fairly quickly from one location to another, and if you use scenery it should be very simple so it can be easily changed without stopping the action of the play. For instance, you could attach cardboard or brown wrapping paper to each side of a small step ladder and paint a different scene or object on each side. Two actors can turn the ladder, changing the tree side to the house side as the action moves from forest to town. Or two extra dancer-actors can do the changing while the actors move into the next scene.

If your audience is not sitting in a circle around the playing space, you might want scenery on the back wall. Cloth panels or window shades with scenes painted on them or patterns glued on them can be very

106

effective. You can roll them up, turn them over, or move them off stage when you want the scene to change. Or you can use simple background pieces like bamboo screens, grass mats, or tie-dyed cloth, which create an interesting background for the playing space without making it look like a specific place.

The stage props you use to sit or stand on can be blocks, chairs, boards, or benches decorated to look like African furniture or things animal characters might use. Burlap cloth, bark, or straw make interesting textures for decoration. Or use neutral pieces like plain blocks, boxes, overturned sturdy wastebaskets which change from a bed to a chair to a wall depending on how they're used by the actors.

Another solution for both stage props and background scenery is to make people scenery. Use your bodies to create benches and trees and walls. Then when the scene needs to change, the scenery changes itself!

COSTUMES

Costumes sometimes help the audience see more clearly who the characters are, and they can also help the actor feel more like the character. But, because you can do these same things through your acting, elaborate costumes aren't really necessary for the plays in this book. Just wear your regular clothes, selecting something that won't get in your way when you move. You might choose something from your wardrobe that seems suitable for the character you're playing, such as a perky, bright outfit for Mr. Hare or old, drab clothes for Wart Hog.

If you want to use costumes, some questions to ask are: What would best show the personality of the character? What colors suit the character? Is she timid or bossy? Is he tricky or wistful? Even though you want your characters to look different, you also want them to look like they're all from the same play. One way to do this is to have everyone wear the same basic outfit, such as jeans and T-shirts or tights and jerseys. Then, to identify each character, just add one or two costume pieces that would be characteristic of the role. Or, you can use masks for everyone—animals and humans alike —with the rest of the body in the same simple outfits. Either of these two methods will make fast costume changes easy. Feet, by the way, can be barefoot or in sandals or sneakers.

SIMPLE COSTUME IDEAS

Basic unit outfits for all characters:
    leotards and tights
    jeans and turtle neck jerseys
    gym shorts and T-shirts
    bathing suits (tank style)

Costume pieces to add to the unit outfits, with color suggestions for character emphasis:

The Man Who Loved to Laugh

Man—in red, with small knitted cap

Wife—in yellow, with head wrap

Chief—in white, with bedspread or sheet (center head-hole cut out) worn as a robe

Bully Snake—in dark green, with masking tape body stripes

Little Snake—in light green, with masking tape body stripes

Dog—in brown, with headband and ears

Rat—in black or gray, with nose piece

Mr. Hare Takes Mr. Leopard for a Ride

Mr. Hare—in orange, with cap and ears

Mr. Leopard—in yellow, with T-shirt with spots that are cut out, pasted on, or colored in, and headband with ears

Mrs. Leopard—in yellow, with shirt like Mr. Leopard's, plus headband with ears

Ananse's Trick Does Double Work

Ananse—in black, with skirt made from raffia or crepe-paper strips, hanging from neck to knees

Goat—in deep pink, with headband with horns and beard

Lion—in rust, with string-mop mane or skull cap with crepe-paper coils

Wart Hog—in brown, with two egg carton bottoms tied on as a breast plate

Turkey—in red, with smooth, plain bathing cap, plus piece of red felt taped to bridge of nose or to sides of throat

Turtle—in yellow-green, with a poncho for shell
Pigeons—in blue or purple, with shawls or bath-
    towels over shoulders, and triangle bandana
    worn backwards over head for beak
Farmer—in rust, with loose, short-sleeved shirt
Boy—in maroon, with loose, short-sleeved shirt
Wife—in blue, with wrap-around skirt

MORE ELABORATE COSTUME SUGGESTIONS

In many West African countries, working men wear cut-off khakis and a straight, loose shirt of home-spun or brightly printed fabric. This shirt is called a *danshiki* (dahn she kee) by the Yoruba people of Ni-geria. On their heads Yoruba men often wear small knitted caps or a little pill-box shaped hat called a *fila* (feé lah). Women often wear a wrap-around dress called an *iro* (eé row) that requires no sewing. The cloth is wrapped around under the arms or at the waist. With a waist wrap you could wear a jersey top or blouse of your own, or make an African-style fitted blouse with shirred peplum. With an *iro*, women have an extra piece of cloth called an *iborun* (ee bór un) draped over one shoulder. They use it to carry their baby on their back or to tie their goods in when they shop. When they dance, they often wave their *iborun* in front of the person they're honoring. Women make a *gele* (géh le) head wrap from a large piece of cloth which is twisted around and tied in grand fashion, or they'll leave their head uncovered and braid their hair in beautiful patterns.

On more dressy occasions, both Yoruba men and women wear long robes. The men's robe is called an *agbada* (ag báh da) and the women's a *buba* (bóo ba). The simplest way to make these robes is by sewing together two huge rectangles of cloth on the top and sides, leaving space for a neck-hole and hand-holes. Robes are fun to dance in, because your movements make big swirls of color.

If you're interested in giving these plays a traditional African feeling, look at photographs and drawings of African dress. See the bibliography on page 123. Talk with people who have lived in Africa, who can give you more details and perhaps show you clothing they have brought from Africa. There are many different ethnic groups in Africa and each one has its own style of traditional dress.

Animal characters can also wear African dress. Mrs. Leopard, for instance, might wear an *iro* dress wrap and have a stocking helmet mask with ears, or she might wear a *gele* head wrap with a leopard face mask. Animals that need to move around quickly, like Rat, Dog, Hare, and Pigeons, could use short waist wraps and little ponchos of fur or feathers and hats or headbands to which ears or feathers are attached.

MASKS

There are many kinds of masks and many ways to make them. Face masks can cover all of your face or can be cut away to leave parts of it free. Helmet masks, which fit over your whole head, can cover your face completely, partially, or not at all. You can make masks from paper, cardboard, cloth, wood, masking tape, papier-maché, or soluble plastics. Paper bags or stocking caps are the easiest materials to use for helmet masks.

Paper Bag Helmet Mask

Glue or staple on paper fringe for mane.

LION

Stocking Cap Helmet Mask

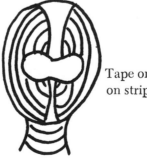

Tape or paint on stripes.

113

SNAKE

Making a Paper Cut-Out Face Mask

LEOPARD

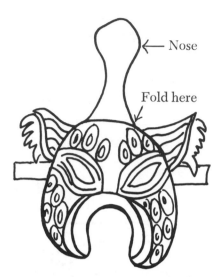

1. Fold paper in half and draw mask shape.

2. Cut out and decorate mask. Decorate back of nose.

3. Fold down nose and glue on paper or straw whiskers.

Some Additional Designs for Paper Cut-Out Face Masks

DOG

GOAT

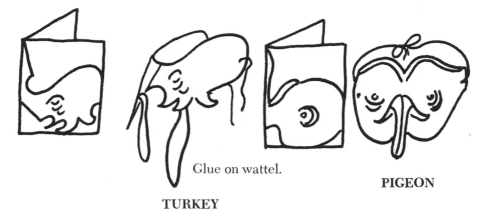

Glue on wattel.

TURKEY

PIGEON

RAT

WARTHOG

To give the masks an African look, study pictures of African masks and sculpture. Notice the basic shapes and the way in which they are decorated. For your own decorations, you can collect and use all kinds of things like straw, nails, egg cartons, bottle caps, string, and macaroni. The illustrations will show you some designs for paper cut-out masks. For more detailed instructions on mask construction check out books on mask making and adapt these designs or make up some of your own. See the bibliography on page 122.

Performing in costumes and masks takes practice. With a mask covering your face, the way you tilt your head and hold your body becomes very important in communicating what the character is feeling and doing. The way you use your body can make the mask seem to smile or scowl. If your mouth is covered, your voice must be especially expressive and loud. Ask others to watch you and let you know if your words and actions are coming across clearly.

Practice wearing your masks and costumes. You want your body to feel as comfortable in the costume as the character would in his or her own clothes or skin. Work in them, refit them if necessary, make sure they will stay on securely and fit your movements, and that your movements fit them. Learn how it is that a turtle gets along with flippers instead of arms and how a person can work in a dress that is only wrapped on. No matter how beautiful the costumes and masks are, remember it is the actor's movements that make the character come alive!

116

SHARING YOUR PLAY
WITH AN AUDIENCE

REHEARSING

To help each other get ready for an audience, be an audience for each other as you work. Your eye is the most valuable aid you can give to your fellow players. So when you aren't performing, watch the others work. Afterward (it's annoying to be interrupted!) have sharing sessions where you tell each other what you saw, and what the performance made you think or feel as you watched. This feedback will help the actor decide whether or not he or she has made the right choices and what sections need more work.

It is not helpful to make comments like "You should have . . ." or "I would have done . . ." Those are ways of trying to make choices for another actor. This isn't fair. Making the choices are part of his creative work and should be respected as his job. On the other hand, letting the actor know how you saw his work and giving your opinion, when asked, can help him or her make good decisions.

Most decisions about individual characters are made by the actors playing those characters. But there are some decisions that need to be made by the group. Group decisions concern the whole production and how the parts are fitting together. When everyone working on the project agrees on the over-all effect, it is easier for each person to fit into the whole. And if everyone is considerate of each other and willing to make changes, you'll be able to balance all the people and their ideas.

Sometimes it helps to have one of the group stay outside each play and be the director. A good director takes part in all the discussions about the play and is the sensitive outside "eye" for the actors as they work, helping them create the effect they want. If you take turns playing parts, you might also take turns being director.

A SPACE FOR PERFORMING

In choosing a performing space, there are two things to keep in mind—the size of the audience you've invited and the space required by the action in the plays. If a small space is best for the feeling of your performance, you'll have to invite fewer people and give more performances. If it's important to have a large audience, then find a large space and put action into your play that will fill a large playing area.

School auditoriums or cafetorium stages can be difficult places for performing because the actors' space is often cold and uninteresting and the audience seems very far away. Think about using regular classrooms or all-purpose rooms in school or your living room and porch at home. Outdoors can be fun, too, because there are so many different shapes to places. It's much harder to be heard outside, so keep the audience small and close or else do a dance or mime show where words aren't important.

Here and on the following page are some ways to arrange the space for performers and audience:

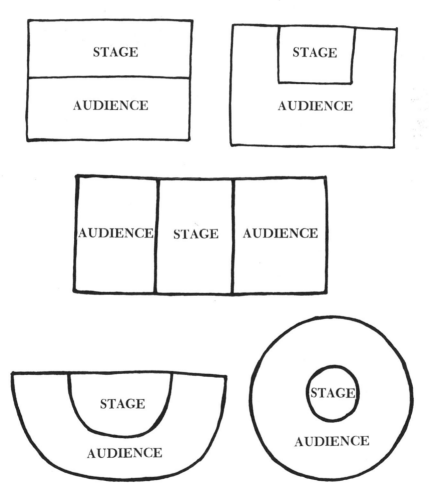

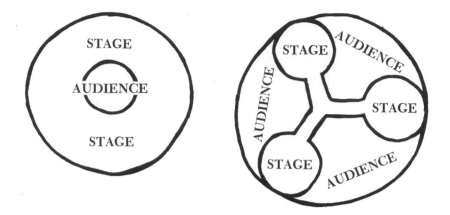

Whatever your playing area, once the audience is sitting in a group that makes them more than three people deep, they'll have trouble seeing. By using platforms, stairways, or combinations of sitting and standing, you can raise the playing area or the viewing area. The simplest solution is usually the best. Just keep in mind that you want a space in which you can be seen and heard by everyone who comes.

PUTTING IT ALL TOGETHER

Once you have worked with as many of these elements as you wish to use—acting, dancing, music, costumes, or scenery—and you have made choices about how you want to use them, give yourself plenty of time to practice putting everything together. You want to make sure that when the parts come together they create the effect you want. You may have to change or rearrange things again. Notice the different speeds you use—the silences, the sounds, the stillness, and the movement. See if the combination created by all these things working together is exciting.

When it's the way you want it, rehearse everything from beginning to end without stopping. Do this enough times to feel sure and natural about what you're doing. These run-through rehearsals, where you don't stop to fix or change anything, are very important. They make everyone aware of the flow of the whole piece. If there are rough spots, work on them after the run-through and then run through it all again.

Your last rehearsals are called dress rehearsals, where you do things exactly as you would if the audience were there. This gives everyone a chance to see if all things are ready. When your mind and your body know instinctively how everything fits together, and you no longer waste energy worrying about what part comes next, you can put yourself fully into the performing and really enjoy it.

The whole process of trying out different things, making choices, and practicing is more than half the fun of working on a play. But there certainly is an added pleasure when you perform for an audience, because then you can share some of those good things with them.

BIBLIOGRAPHY

AFRICAN FOLKTALES FOR CHILDREN

AARDEMA, VERNA. *Tales from the Story Hat.* (New York: Coward-McCann, 1960.

BURTON, W.F.R. *The Magic Drum.* New York: Criterion Books, 1961.

COURLANDER, HAROLD. *The Hat-Shaking Dance and Other Tales from the Gold Coast.* New York: Harcourt, Brace, 1957.

COURLANDER, HAROLD, and HERZOG, GEORGE. *The Cowtail Switch and Other Stories.* New York: Henry Holt, 1957.

ELLIOT, GERALDINE. *The Hunter's Cave.* Boston: Robert Bentley, 1953.

HEADY, ELEANOR. *Safiri the Singer: East African Tales.* Chicago: Follett, 1972.

PRICE, PATTIE. *Bantu Tales.* New York: E.P. Dutton, 1938.

SHERLOCK, PHILIP. *Anansi, the Spider Man, Jamaican Folk Tales.* New York: Thomas Y. Crowell, 1954.

STURTON, HUGH. *Zomo, the Rabbit.* New York: Atheneum, 1966.

WALKER, BARBARA. *The Dancing Palm Tree and Other Nigerian Folktales.* New York: Parents Magazine Press, 1968.

AFRICAN SCULPTURE AND MASKS

DUERDEN, DENNIS. *African Art.* London: Hamlyn, 1968.
    Excellent photographs of traditional African masks, including some photos of people wearing them in ceremonies; map showing location of the ethnic groups represented.

GLUBOK, SHIRLEY. *The Art of Africa.* New York: Harper and Row, 1965.
    Photographs of masks and sculpture.

RADIN, PAUL, editor. *African Folktales and Sculpture.* Bollingen
Series XXXII, Pantheon Books, Random House. Kingsport, Tenn.: Kingsport Press, 1964.

Many large photographs of African sculpture, doz-
ens of folktales in direct translation from original versions;
map showing location of the ethnic groups represented.

WILLETT, FRANK. *African Art: An Introduction.* New York: Prae-
ger, 1971.

Many photographs and drawings of sculpture,
masks, objects, fabric design, and styles of traditional
buildings from cultural groups throughout Africa.

AFRICAN PEOPLE IN TRADITIONAL CLOTHING

BERNHEIM, MARC and EVELYN. *From Bush to City: A Look at the
New Africa,* revised edition. New York: Harcourt, Brace,
and World, 1968.

Text and photographs of African people in villages
and cities.

_____. *In Africa.* New York: Atheneum, 1973.

Text and photographs showing African people from
many different countries wearing many different styles of
clothing.

ELISOFON, ELIOT. "Africa's Ancient Splendor Still Gleams in the
Akan People's Golden Art." *The Smithsonian,* January,
1973.

Article containing many beautiful color photographs of traditional dress and customs of the Ashanti people in Ghana.

ENGLEBERT, VICTOR. *Camera on Ghana: The World of a Young
Fisherman.* New York: Harcourt, Brace, Jovanovich,
1971.

Text and photographs focusing on daily life of a young boy in a fishing village.

FEELINGS, TOM. *Black Pilgrimage.* New York: Lothrop, Lee, and Shepard, 1972.

Personal account of Mr. Feelings's discovery of his African roots; some beautiful illustrations of African dress.

ACTING FOR CHILDREN

OLFSON, LEWY. *You Can Act.* New York: Sterling, 1971.

Good ideas for making up your own plays and scenes, pantomiming, making up dialogue, masks, puppets, chorus work, sound effects; good notes to adults who might help you.

SMITH, MOYNE R. *Plays and How to Put Them On.* New York: Walck, 1961.

A good introductory chapter on how to make up and rehearse plays; second chapter on technical aspects of putting on plays: costumes, scenery, and make-up.

DRAMA WORKSHOPS FOR ADULT LEADERS

SPOLIN, VIOLA. *Improvisation for the Theatre.* Evanston, Illinois: Northwestern University Press, 1963.

Hundreds of theater games and discussion of principles behind game structure for improvisation work.

WARD, WINIFRED. *Playmaking with Children,* New York: Appleton Century, 1947.

Some very useful pointers on using stories as the point of departure in creative drama work.

WAY, BRIAN. *Development Through Drama.* New York: Humanities Press, 1972.

Excellent text for teachers and leaders who are

124

inexperienced in drama; clear presentation of philosophy with many specific exercises.

COSTUMES

BERK, BARBARA. *The First Book of Stage Costume and Make-Up.* New York: Franklin Watts, 1954.

A very easy "how to" book on collecting, adapting, and/or making costumes; mask and animal ideas.

CUMMINGS, RICHARD. *101 Costumes for All Ages, All Occasions.* New York: Van Rees Press, 1971.

Instructions for making easy and advanced costumes, novelty costumes; principles of design.

PARISH, PEGGY. *Costumes to Make.* (London: The Macmillan Co., Collier-Macmillian Ltd., 1970.

A simple guide to cutting out, sewing, or glueing costumes for specific characters; section on animals.

PURDY, SUSAN. *Costumes You Can Make.* New York: J.B. Lippincott, 1971.

Illustrations and instructions for beginning cutting, sewing, dyeing, painting, and trimming—simple and complicated versions; special suggestions for animals and masks.

WISEMAN, ANN. *Making Things: The Handbook of Creative Discovery.* Boston: Little, Brown, 1973.

Ideas and instructions for making tons of things, including: jewelry, batik dyeing, tie dyeing, simple robes, grass hats, grass mats, foot gloves, box costumes, sock and finger puppets, and an East African thumb piano.

MASK MAKING

ALKEMA, CHESTER JAY. *Masks.* New York: Sterling, 1971.
> Many different ways of making masks including papier-mâché and paper cut-outs; exciting photographs of masks.

CUMMINGS, RICHARD. *101 Masks.* New York: David McKay, 1968.
> Many illustrations for masks from very simple to professional methods; many different characters and different theatrical styles shown; make-up ideas.

D'AMATO, JANET and ALEX. *African Crafts for You to Make.* New York: Julian Messner, 1969.
> Drawings of masks, sculpture, props, games from many African cultures; information about the culture and instructions for making the objects.

MUSIC

CATHERALL, E.A., and HOLT, P.N., *Working with Sounds.* Chicago: Albert Whitman, 1964.
> Ideas for making sounds from instruments and objects that aren't instruments.

HAWKINSON, JOHN, and FAULHABER, MARTHA. *Music and Instruments for Children to Make,* Book One. Chicago: Albert Whitman, 1971.
> A beginning book about sound and rhythm; instructions for making and using very simple instruments.

————. *Rhythms, Music, and Instruments to Make,* Book Two. Chicago: Albert Whitman, 1971.
> Rhythms to walk and drum; instructions for making rhythm instruments, flutes, metallophones, xylophones, box harp, guitar, and violin.

126

WARREN, FRED. *The Music of Africa: An Introduction.* Englewood Cliffs, N.J.: Prentice-Hall, 1970.

Excellent illustrations and descriptions of African musical instruments and African music; long list of records of African music.

WOOD, ROBERT, and MANDELL, MURIEL. *Make Your Own Musical Instruments.* New York: Sterling, 1959.

Instructions and illustrations for making many different musical instruments from inexpensive materials.

DISCOGRAPHY

African Tribal Music and Dances. Sonar Seghor Ak Sicco Yi, Counterpoint/CPT 5513, Esoteric Recors, 1313 N. Vine St., Hollywood.

Dinizulu Troup Sings Songs of West Africa. Continental Records, 500 Fifth Avenue, N.Y.

The Drums of Dinizulu, Dinizulu African Troupe, Songs of Ghana and Anago Chants. Afrotone, STLP 700.

Drums of the Yoruba of Nigeria. Ethnic Folkways Library FE 4441.

Music of Equatorial Africa. Ethnic Folkways Library FE 4402.

Music of the Jos Plateau and other Regions of Nigeria. Ethnic Folkways Library FE 4321.

Olatunji: Drums of Passion. Columbia, CS 9310.

Olatunji: More Drums of Passion. Columbia, CS 9307.

Voices of Africa: High Life and Other Popular Music. Saka Acquare and his African Ensemble from Ghana, Nonesuch Explorer Series H–72026.

Wolof Music of Senegal and the Gambia. Ethnic Folkways Library FE 4462.

ABOUT THE AUTHOR

CAROL KORTY received her B.A. in theater from Antioch College and her M.A. from Sarah Lawrence College. She was Director of Children's Theater at the State University of New York, Brockport, for five years and is now an Associate Professor of theater at the University of Massachusetts in Amherst. She has danced professionally in New York City and on national tour in musical comedy, opera, and modern dance. In connection with her work with children's theater, she has received three Title I grants and two New York State Council on the Arts grants. She has conducted numerous teacher training workshops in drama and has taught creative drama and dance to children in camps, settlement houses, and public schools. She is currently holding weekly drama classes for young people at the Amherst Ballet Center.

J812   K84   534-76

Korty

PLAYS FROM AFRICAN FOLKTALES

DATE DUE